WYMONDHAM

HISTORY OF A NORFOLK MARKET TOWN

Wymondham Market Cross c. 1807 by Robert Dixon

WYMONDHAM

HISTORY OF A NORFOLK MARKET TOWN

edited by

MARY GARNER
JOHN WILSON

WYMONDHAM HERITAGE SOCIETY

Wymondham, Norfolk

2006

First published for the
WYMONDHAM HERITAGE SOCIETY,
10, The Bridewell, Norwich Road, Wymondham, Norfolk, NR18 0NS
Registered charity No. 299548
2006

ISBN: 1-901553-03-5
978-1-901553-03-1

British Library Cataloguing-in-Publication Data
A catalogue record for this book is available from the British Library

Printed and bound in Great Britain by
Print Services,
University of East Anglia,
Norwich, NR4 7TJ

Contents

List of Illustrations

Acknowledgements

The authors of this book owe a special debt of gratitude to *Christopher Barringer*, a leading figure among local historians in Norfolk. He is currently Chairman of the Dragon Hall Education Committee and was formerly Director of Extra-Mural Studies at the Centre of Continuing Education at the University of East Anglia. He has stimulated, encouraged and inspired many to study local history, including those involved in writing this book. It was a group led by Chris which researched and wrote *Wymondham in the Seventeenth Century.*

Acknowledgements and thanks are also due to many other people, including the staff of the Norfolk Heritage Centre, the Norfolk Archive Centre, the Norfolk Museums and Archaeology Service, *Janet Smith* of the Wymondham Town Archive and *Paul Cattermole* of the Wymondham Parish Records.

The authors are all members of the Wymondham Heritage Society and experienced local history researchers. They are:

John Ayton, a retired county planning officer, is the long-standing editor of *The Annual* published by Norfolk Archaeological and Historical Research Group (NAHRG).

Richard Fowle, a solicitor, both contributed to and co-edited an earlier publication, *Wymondham in the Seventeenth Century.*

Mary Garner, a former civil servant, has obtained, in retirement, a Certificate and Diploma in Local History, and also a Certificate in Landscape History, from the University of East Anglia. She is assistant archivist at Wymondham Town Archive.

Adrian Hoare, a retired history teacher, has published various books on local history, including *An Unlikely Rebel: Robert Kett and the Norfolk Rising* 1549.

Mark Phillips is an accountant in local government who has researched various aspects of Wymondham's history.

Norma Virgoe is a historian who has published several books on various aspects of Norfolk history, including *Halls of Zion: Chapels and Meeting Houses in Norfolk* (jointly with Janet Ede and Tom Williamson).

John Wilson, a retired history teacher, has edited *Wymondham Inventories 1590–1641,* contributed local history articles to NAHRG's *The Annual* and edited the text of the *'Wymondham Town Book 1585–1620'* for volume LXX (2006) of the *Norfolk Record Society* series.

Foreword

In 1949 J E G Mosby and P E Agar wrote *Wymondham Old and New*. Since then no attempt has been made to tell the story of Wymondham's long and interesting history. With this volume, edited by Mary Garner and John Wilson, we have a group of well qualified researchers who have combined to give us the history of the town. It is a daunting challenge, we have the story from the ice ages to the latest changes taking place in the town now, the whole of which is enlivened with nearly seventy well chosen illustrations.

All sorts of especially interesting items are included. The best account as yet given of the way the great manor of Grishaugh worked is presented. A vivid picture of a Tudor yeoman, Philip Cullyer, a local benefactor, is drawn. A view of Robert Kett as an important figure of Wymondham, before the famous rising, creates a sympathetic picture of a future 'rebel'.

Wymondham's early records and those surviving after the dissolution of the Abbey are remarkable and the extracts from the Town Book, especially those relating to the fire of 1615, are fascinating.

Into the eighteenth century the picture of agriculture revealed by the life of Randall Burroughes, the remarkable census of 1747 by Mr Cremer and the occupation lists of Mr Petit, two Wymondham vicars, gives us a description of Wymondham's economy in that period. A third vicar, William Papillon, saved the wonderful views of the Abbey by preserving the meadows around it. The later accounts of 'the chattering looms', of the 19th century growth of industries and of the many changes in the 20th century give us a vivid portrait of the growing town and of its newly enclosed surroundings.

Overall we are presented with a well researched, well illustrated picture of one of Norfolk's most important market towns. The team and its editors are to be congratulated on its production.

Chris Barringer

CHAPTER ONE

Early Wymondham

Geology

Wymondham is situated nine miles south-west of Norwich and lies on the central and southern Norfolk boulder clays. These were deposited by the last Ice Age over the underlying chalk and also include gravels and flints as well as clay. There is no useful building stone locally so flint has provided the materials for many of the

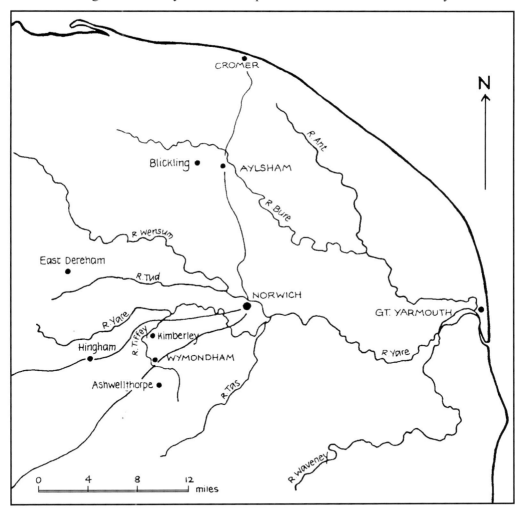

1. Wymondham location map.

local buildings. Wymondham is situated near the central north-south watershed which divides Norfolk and is traversed by the River Tiffey which flows in a north-westerly direction to join with the River Yare which then flows east into the North Sea. Originally this central area of Norfolk was well-wooded, but it was gradually cleared over the centuries. The parish of Wymondham has an area of 10,484 acres (4,243 hectares), far larger than any other in Norfolk save Methwold on the edge of the Fens.

Early History

There is no documentary evidence of Wymondham's history until the Domesday Book was written in 1086, so the early history has to be gathered from the archaeological record and interpretation of the findings of research in Norfolk generally. The chief archaeological methods used in Wymondham have been field walking and metal-detecting, but, because these have not been applied to the whole parish, the resulting evidence is somewhat fragmentary. In addition, the town itself probably covers traces of early evidence with later. However, in 2005 an archaeological excavation near Browick Road produced artefacts from the Neolithic Age through to the medieval period, showing that there had been activity and occupation in the area for thousands of years. Examples of archaeological finds in the area can be seen in the Wymondham Heritage Museum and a record of all archaeological finds is kept by Norfolk Landscape Archaeology at Gressenhall and can be viewed by appointment. The comments below on the early landscape are based on research that has been carried out in Norfolk in general.

From the Ice Age to the Iron Age

When the climate warmed after the last Ice Age, the country gradually became covered in trees, first birch, willow and pine, then from about 8500 BC by hazel, elm, oak and lime. This ancient woodland began to be cleared by man when farming was introduced in the Neolithic period, from about 4000 BC, but it was a very gradual process.

There is archaeological evidence of man in Wymondham from all periods of prehistory. There are Palaeolithic and Mesolithic hand-axes and flints left by the hunter-gatherers during the ice-ages and later. Farming started in the Neolithic period onwards leaving axe heads, arrow-heads and evidence of flint-working. The Bronze Age lasted from 2350 BC until 800 BC and the introduction of metal-working left bronze axe heads as well as more flint workings, plus pottery. In addition, Bronze Age burial sites in the form of ring-ditches have been found through aerial photography.

During the Iron Age (*c.*800 BC–AD 43) there was the gradual development of the so-called 'Celtic' landscape of small fields, ditches and tracks. Pollen analyses from Norfolk meres have shown herbaceous plants rapidly increasing at the expense of trees, confirming the continuing clearance of trees and increase in farming. A tribe called the Iceni gradually became dominant, and coins came into use towards the end of the period. The most important Iron Age site in Wymondham was found in Silfield when the new by-pass was being built in the 1990s. This site appeared to be a settlement and industrial site, with evidence of iron-working as well as flint work and antler carving.

The Roman period (AD 43 to AD 410)

Apart from a few coins and other items, there is little evidence of Roman occupation in Wymondham, the main Roman town in Norfolk being *Venta Icenorum* a few miles away to the east (Caistor St Edmund). However, there was a Roman road which ran across Norfolk from Denver to Venta via Threxton and Crownthorpe and there are traces of this road crossing the Downham area of Wymondham. Crownthorpe is a small parish bordering Wymondham to the north-west and a small settlement associated with a Romano-Celtic temple has been found there by archaeologists. There must have been Romano-British farmers living and working in the Wymondham area, but their settlements are unknown, except for an archaeological excavation near Browick Road in 2005 which produced evidence of a Romano-British wooden aisled building, possibly a farm. There is no good building stone in Norfolk so houses would mostly have been built of wood, leaving little evidence.

The Anglo-Saxons

The two-hundred year period after the departure of the Romans in AD 410 was truly a 'Dark Age' and we can only speculate about much of what happened then. Roman town life appears to have collapsed and the country was infiltrated by pagan Germanic peoples and culture. In Norfolk these people included Angles and Frisians from Denmark, north Germany and northern Holland whose language totally replaced the British and Latin previously spoken. The pollen record shows that farming continued and the woodland did not regenerate so there could not have been a long period when society totally broke down, as used to be thought. This new society formed small independent tribal territories which later, as the Anglo-Saxon kingdoms evolved, gradually merged and a pattern of large royal estates were established within the East Anglian kingdom. Eventually, in their turn many of these estates gradually split into smaller units forming the manors found in the Domesday Book in the eleventh century. However, this division does not appear to have occurred in Wymondham which remained as a royal estate and one manor until after the Norman Conquest. Anglo-Saxon archaeological remains dating from the early sixth century onwards have been found in Wymondham.

The origin of the name 'Wymondham' is of Anglo-Saxon origin and probably consists of a personal name, such as Wigmund, plus 'ham' meaning village or settlement. 'Ham' names tended to be places in the core area of an estate and are often attached to early personal names, such as Wigmund. An earlier explanation that the name meant the village on a pleasant mount, 'win-munte-ham', has been discounted. The name is pronounced 'Windum' and was frequently spelled as 'Windham' in old documents.

As stated earlier, Wymondham has an area of almost 11,000 acres (4,243 hectares) which is much larger than the vast majority of parishes in Norfolk. There is evidence that Wymondham was administered as four areas, known as divisions or 'shifts', being Norton, Suton, Silfield and Wattlefield. These divisions seem to pre-date the progressive split of the single Manor of Wymondham into several different manors during the mediaeval period.

Christianity

Christianity arrived in Norfolk during the seventh century. Early ecclesiastical organisation was based on larger areas than the later parishes and consisted of a minster church with a team of priests to serve the area. Although the sites of these minsters are difficult to establish in Norfolk, it is believed that many were based on the royal estates mentioned earlier, Wymondham being one of them. The pattern of parishes in Norfolk may well indicate the site of these minsters, with one central parish surrounded by a ring of attached parishes. This pattern occurs at North Walsham, Aylsham and Wymondham, and can be seen in the attached map of Wymondham (*Fig. 2, p. 5*).

Parishes developed during the tenth and eleventh centuries as wealthy landowners decided to build their own churches and the minster organisation gradually broke down, but for some reason, probably that the parish remained in royal hands, Wymondham never split up into smaller parishes. Traces of an earlier Anglo-Saxon church have been found in an archaeological investigation under the east tower of the present church, showing that the church in Wymondham has probably always been on the same site on the hill above the river.

The Danes

By the beginning of the ninth century both Norwich and Thetford were thriving towns and Wymondham was on the route between them, probably a successful farming community, with a minster church of some kind. However, from 800 the Danes started raiding England. These raids increased after 835 and from 851 they were over-wintering in camps rather than returning to Denmark. In 869 they spent the winter at Thetford and killed the last East Anglian king, Edmund (later canonised) which must have caused much fear and panic throughout the region. For the next fifty years East Anglia was under Danish control. It is not known how many settled here in this period but they gradually were converted to Christianity and learned to speak English. The archaeological remains left by the Danes are scant, but their presence is revealed in place-names, such as those with names ending in 'by' and 'thorpe', and also in some other words such as 'gata' which means 'street'. In Wymondham this is reflected in the name of Damgate.

Later Anglo-Saxon period

In 917 the Danes were defeated by Edmund the Elder, king of Wessex and son of Alfred the Great. From this date onwards East Anglia was part of the kingdom of Wessex and eventually the whole of England. Edmund set up new units as sub-

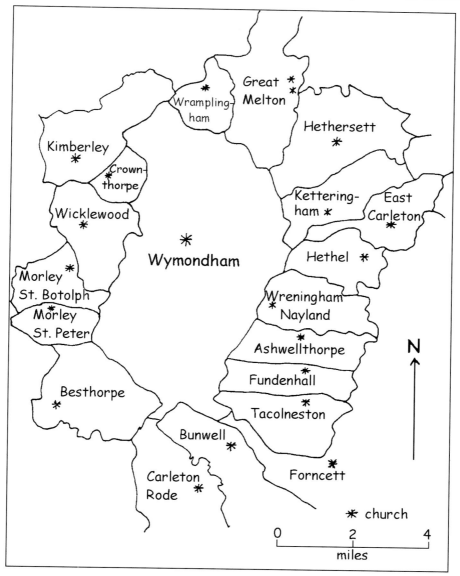

2. The dominant size of Wymondham among its surrounding parishes.

5

divisions of the counties to administer taxation, justice and military service called 'Hundreds' of which Norfolk contained thirty-three. These hundreds continued in their administrative function until the nineteenth century (albeit with changes over the years). Wymondham was in the Hundred of Forehoe which eventually consisted of twenty-four parishes including Hingham and Costessey as well as Wymondham. Wymondham was regarded as a half-hundred in its own right due to its size, which gave it an element of independence.

One factor that should be remembered from this period onwards is the presence only nine miles away of the thriving trading centre of Norwich, which created marketing opportunities for many surrounding settlements including Wymondham, as well as providing a centre of administration.

By the end of the tenth century, the Danes returned. They were paid off with Danegeld (enormous sums of money raised by taxation) several times by the king, Ethelred the Unready. However, they returned in 1004 and sacked both Norwich and Thetford, bringing more death and destruction to Norfolk, possibly including Wymondham as it was on the route between the two towns. In 1012 the east of England became part of the Danish empire and from 1015 Canute (or Cnut) was king, from 1016 king of all England. Later, this empire split up and England was once more ruled by Saxons: Edward the Confessor (1042–1066) and Harold. However, in 1066 the country was successfully invaded by William, Duke of Normandy, and his followers.

CHAPTER TWO

The Middle Ages

The Norman Conquest

At the time of the invasion in 1066, Wymondham was under the authority of Stigand, the Archbishop of Canterbury since 1052, and was a prosperous farming community with a church and possibly a market (although there are no records of this until later). Apart from its royal connection, it was on the direct route and on a river crossing between the two major Saxon settlements of Thetford and Norwich. The Domesday Book shows that the township was initially awarded to Ralph Guader (or de Gaël), Earl of Norfolk and Suffolk. However, in 1075 he joined a rebellion against King William. This rebellion was rapidly put down which forced Ralph to retreat from Cambridge to Norwich before escaping abroad. During his retreat it is believed he and his army stopped in his estate of Wymondham, slaughtering many of the oxen here for food, thus possibly explaining the reduction in the number of plough teams from 1066 to 1086.

After the rebellion and until after the completion of the Domesday Book, the estate was once more held by the king, with part being held by William de Warenne, another great lord. Dykebeck was listed as separate settlement and was held by Ralph Baynard, as was another small settlement, Hidichethorp, which Ralph Baynard had seized without permission. The estate of Wymondham was subsequently awarded by the king to William d'Albini, a member of the royal household, of whom more details are given below.

Besides the great changes caused in society due to the introduction of the French-speaking nobility, there were also changes in the landscape, including the building of castles and many new churches. In Wymondham, Moot Hill is a wooded mound on the edge of Kett's Park next to the new by-pass. Archaeologists believe this to be a Norman ringwork, which would have been topped by a wooden fortress, built shortly after the Conquest, but soon abandoned.

The Normans developed deer-parks, some of which were stocked with fallow deer (a new introduction from abroad). A deer-park was established in the Silfield area of Wymondham; the hedge and ditch surrounding it can still be seen in places (*see fig. 4, p. 11*) and its outline is clear on maps. The Normans also introduced rabbits, which were initially delicate animals kept in warrens built especially for them. Many of these warrens were in Breckland, but records show there was one within the hunting park. (Pheasants were also a medieval introduction).

7

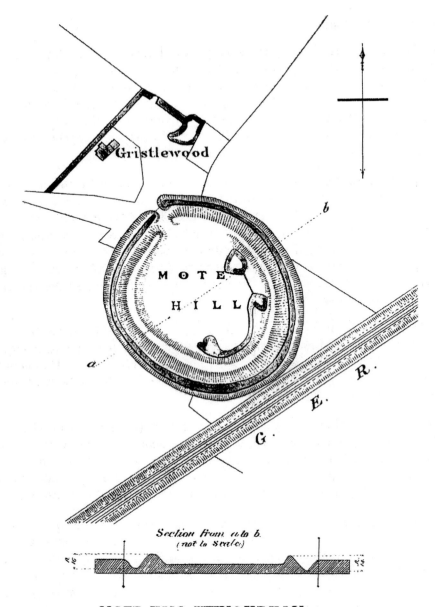

Gristlewood

M O T E

H I L L

a

b

G . E . R .

Section from a to b.
(not to scale)

MOTE HILL, WYMONDHAM.
From the Ordnance Survey by permission of Capt.ⁿ Day R.E.

Scale of Chains.

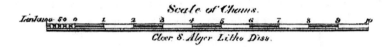

Clerk S. Alger Litho Diss.

3. *Plan and cross-section of Moot Hill (Norfolk Archaeology, Vol. IX, 1884).*

The Domesday Book

King William ordered the great survey now known as the Domesday Book at Christmas 1085, twenty years after the Conquest. By August 1086 the initial results were already being collated. Primarily, the survey was a record of all the landholders and their estates in England, and also a record of the equivalent information in 1066 before the Conquest. The purpose of the survey is unclear, but it acted as both a land register and also a taxation aid. Historians still have some problems with the terminology and statistics used.

Early documentary sources for Norfolk are rare due to the destruction of land charters and other documents by the Danes in raids on monasteries and other places. The Domesday Book is therefore the first documentary record for many places in Norfolk, including Wymondham. Entries in the Domesday Book for Essex, Norfolk and Suffolk are contained in what is known as 'the Little Domesday Book' which is more detailed than the entries in the other, larger, book covering the rest of the country. Even so, the entry for Wymondham is still rather confusing and unclear.

The Wymondham Domesday entry for the main Wymondham holding states that by 1086 there were 130 sokemen (freemen who were connected to manors), while tied to the landholding were 64 villagers (or villeins), 174 smallholders (cottars) and 8 slaves (serfs), making a total of 376 men in the settlement and a total population of about 1,500 people.

There were 4 ploughteams on the lord's own farm (demesne) and 52 ploughteams on the lands held by the men. These figures indicate that there was a considerable amount of arable land in the community. However, the number of ploughteams was considerably higher, 88, in 1066. The Domesday entry states this loss was caused by Earl Ralph's rebellion, but also says that 'all could be restored'.

In the Little Domesday Book, woodland was measured by a notional number of pigs that could be kept there. In Wymondham in 1086 there was woodland for 94 pigs. However, in 1066 there had been woods for 178 pigs, so a considerable amount of woodland had disappeared in the intervening twenty years. (Perhaps partially used on the building of the fort on Moot Hill?) Woodland was very important as it was a managed and renewable resource used for buildings, hedging, tools and implements, as well as fuel.

There were ninety-nine acres of meadow. This also was important, as the hay grown there provided food for the overwintering of animals.

There were six mills: these would have been watermills at this time, as windmills were first recorded in 1191 at Bury St Edmunds. There was also one fishery. Both these facts seem to indicate the river was deeper than now (The priory, founded in

1107, had extensive fishponds.).

Also reported were 2 horses (cobs), 16 cattle, 50 pigs and 24 sheep. This cannot be the total number of animals kept and may be only those held on the demesne farm.

Hidichethorp had twenty-four freemen. There were four ploughteams and five acres of meadow. William de Warenne's separate holding consisted of forty-three freemen and six smallholders. There were two ploughteams (reduced from five in 1066) and six acres of meadow.

Dykebeck had one villein and four cottars, making a total of five men, and around 20 people altogether. There were two ploughteams belonging to the lord and four to the men. There was no woodland (either in 1066 or 1086), four acres of meadow, one cob, four cattle, 22 pigs and 40 sheep. The number of sheep had increased considerably in twenty years, from five in 1066.

Dykebeck was also reported as holding one quarter of a church. Churches were not always mentioned in Domesday Book and it is known there were very many others not reported (as in the entry for Wymondham). Fractions of holdings showed that a property, such as a church, was held by more than one landholder, but where was the rest in this case? This is not known, but could, of course, have belonged to the Wymondham manor itself.

Another omission (apart from the churches) was the lack of mention generally of pasture, essential for the grazing of stock. The reason for this omission is not known. In Wymondham, and much of Norfolk, a considerable amount of the grazing land was provided by the commons.

The Commons

According to the landscape historian, Tom Williamson, most commons in Norfolk evolved before the Norman Conquest from woodland into wood pasture and then, as the trees disappeared, into open common land. In documents the commons were often referred to as 'the common waste'. Contrary to popular belief not everyone had 'common rights', i.e. the right to use the commons: the 'rights' were only attached to certain properties.

The commons were an integral and important part of the farming economy, providing pasture for cattle, sheep and horses, turf and furze for fuel, and clay and sand for building materials. The commons were administered by the manorial lords and the number of animals grazing on them was limited to prevent over-grazing. In general, outsiders straying on to the commons which they were not entitled to use were brought before the manorial courts and fined. However, there is at least one example of outsiders being allowed to use the commons. A document from 1465 shows that two hundred cattle, previously fattened in the area round Ely, were pastured at Wymondham prior to sale in Norwich.

The commons almost surrounded Wymondham: they lay around the border of the parish, outside the town and the fields, and connected with commons in other parishes. They were bordered by hedges, ditches and gates to prevent animals straying on to the arable fields. The acreage of the commons at the time of Domesday is not known, but despite considerable encroachment over the years, there were still about three thousand acres of common in Wymondham in the seventeenth century.

4. Aerial view of the hunting park, Silfield, which can be recognised by its distinctive fan-shaped outline.

Open Fields

Apart from the castles, churches and deer parks, another noticeable change occurred to the local landscape in the early medieval period. This was the change from the earlier small fenced fields to large open ones divided into strips allocated to different farmers in the community. The classic area for this change was in the Midlands and occurred in the late Saxon period. In Norfolk it is believed to have happened later, after the Norman Conquest, possibly due to population pressure and it was never as rigidly organised as in the Midlands. The charter establishing the priory in 1107 mentioned three fields; in Northfield, East field and Silfield, so there were certainly three open fields in Wymondham by that date.

Wymondham eventually acquired several open fields, although the exact number is not clear. There were at least eight in the fourteenth century, spread around the parish, including North Field, Bixland Field, East Field and Stanfield amongst others. Allocation of the strips amongst the various manors is not known: it was certainly not restricted to one manor, one field.

The d'Albini family

The d'Albini family (name Latinised from d'Aubigny) came from the town of St Martin d'Aubigny in the departement of Manche at the lower end of the Cherbourg peninsula in France. The names d'Albini and d'Aubigny seem to have been interchangeable.

William d'Albini was born around 1070. According to some sources, his grandfather, William d'Albini, was a companion of William the Conqueror at the Battle of Hastings on 14th October 1066 and would have been about 56 years old. His father, Roger, then in his late twenties may also have accompanied them although he is not recorded as having been in the battle.

William d'Albini was married to Maud Bigot, the daughter of another Norman lord, and was awarded a considerable dowry for her by King Henry I, including extensive lands as well as the state office of *Pincerna Regis,* i.e. Butler to the King, which included organising royal coronation banquets.

Amongst the many lands William acquired were Old Buckenham, which was his main 'honour' or centre, and Wymondham where he founded the Priory (see below). Both William, who died in 1139, and his wife were buried there in front of the high altar.

William's son, another William, was born about 1109 and also became an important member of the royal household. After the death of Henry I, this William married the king's widow, Adeliza, and was created Earl of Arundel by King Stephen. He built the castle at New Buckenham with the attached planned town and in 1174 founded Becket's Chapel in Wymondham (for details of this see below). He, too, was buried in the Priory founded by his father, as were later members of the family.

The Priory and then the Abbey

In 1107 William d'Albini set up a religious foundation on the site of the earlier Saxon church. It was intended that the foundation should consist of buildings that would serve as a priory with a prior and twelve monks known as regular clergy or 'regulars' and as a parish church for the town with a vicar and clergy known as secular clergy or 'seculars'.

William's brother Richard was the Abbot of St Albans and thus Wymondham Priory was created as a dependency of St Albans. However, instead of awarding the power of appointing the prior to the Abbot of St Albans, as would have been normal, this was reserved to the regulars. They would choose one of their number to be the prior and present him to the founder or patron for his approval although he could not unreasonably refuse their choice. In the foundation deed confirmed by the foundation charter of Henry I, the power to appoint the vicar was conferred on the prior and the monks instead of the lord of the manor as would have been more normal. This arrangement meant that the vicar was responsible for ministering to the townspeople and was answerable to the bishop, but was, nevertheless, reliant on the monks who appointed him.

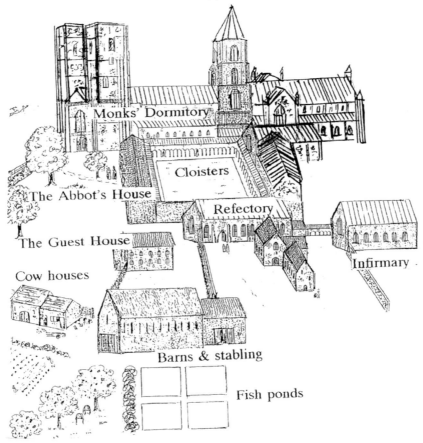

5. *Artist's impression of the later phase of the monastic buildings, 1175–1400.*

The result of these two unusual arrangements was to create a situation that was to lead to endless arguments for years to come. The monks who claimed responsibility of the whole building were answerable only to the prior and resented visitations from the bishop. The Priory was well provided for, being endowed with a third of the Wymondham Manor by its founder and being further provided with the Manor of Happisburgh including 'all wrecks on that part of the coast lying between Eccles, Happisburgh and Tunstead', a marsh in Reedham and a rent of two thousand eels per year from Hillgay in the Fens. This wealth must also have enhanced the monks' feelings of their own importance whilst deepening their resentment at being restrained by the vicar and the bishop.

The Priory seems to have been completed in 1130 since in that year Nigel was appointed as the first prior. Initially the vicar seems to have been one of the monks acting as a chaplain and it was not until 1221 that the first proper vicar, Walter, was appointed. William de Buckenham was appointed in 1234 and at last a secure income was settled.

During the construction of the Priory, the nature of Wymondham must have changed substantially. The construction of a large religious foundation (perhaps similar in size to the abbey we can see at Ely today) must have required the employment of a large number of masons and other craftsmen over a twenty-year period. There would have been continuous arrivals of stone and other building materials as well as visits from dignitaries of all sorts. All these people would have required accommodation and services, and the result must have been to rapidly turn a small Anglo-Saxon village into a very busy Norman town.

Becket's Chapel

Some forty years after the completion of the Priory, Thomas Becket, Archbishop of Canterbury was murdered and two years later in 1172 was canonized. Two years after that William d'Albini, Earl of Arundel, built a chapel and dedicated it to the Virgin Mary and St Thomas Becket. It was well endowed and two monks served there. The religious Guild of St Thomas was founded in 1187 and the members maintained a light at the altar. At the time it was thatched, but in 1400 was rebuilt and re-roofed with a hammer beam roof. There was also a small steeple with bells, which were rung at times of emergency such as fires in the town. The chapel continued as a guild chapel until the Reformation.

Becket's Chapel originally stood in an open space, which, according to the Wymondham Abbey Register, seems to have been the original market place. Although encroached upon and used for many purposes, the Chapel still stands today, housing the town's library, at the junction of Middleton Street, Damgate Street, Market Street and Church Street.

6. Becket's Chapel, drawn by Thomas Jeckyll in 1871 shortly before its restoration, showing how smaller buildings had accrued around its walls by this date, including the shop at the east end, a lock-up and the fire-engine shed.

The Priory: disputes and developments

Disputes arising from the original charter continued to erupt with the regulars claiming jurisdiction over the whole of the monastery including the church itself and the seculars and the town seeking to preserve their control through the vicar. Eventually this resulted in a referral in 1249 to the papal court in Rome where Pope Innocent IV decided that the areas of responsibility within the church should be set out. It should be remembered that the church then was twice its present length being 245 feet long from east to west and without the dividing wall behind the present day altar. The pope decreed that the regulars should have the choir, the transepts, the south aisle and the south-west tower (there then being two squat towers at the western end of the church). The seculars should have control of the parish church which should consist of the nave, the north-west tower and the north aisle and there should be a separate access to the common street.

After the death of William d'Albini, the founder, the Abbot of St Albans evidently felt himself freed from some of the control that the d'Albinis exercised and in 1300 took upon himself the power of appointing the prior which led to much argument with the legitimate patrons.

During the following century the monks carried on building and enlarging their priory and during this period the cloisters were begun and the chapter house was built (the east end still remains). The monks also built a dormitory over the south aisle although they probably already had one somewhere in the area of the chapter house. The new dormitory was provided with 'squints' through which the monks could keep a constant eye on what was going on in the church. Certainly all these activities kept alive the antagonism between the monks and the town.

At the end of the fourteenth century the monks decided to replace their lantern tower which was showing signs of becoming dangerous. In order to house the bells from this tower while they built another, they installed them in the parishioners' tower, which was at the west end of the north aisle. To replace the lantern tower they built a new octagonal tower which today stands at the east end of the building. The new tower was built in a very substantial manner but, it was said, in order to make it secure enough a two-metre wall was built right across the nave. Thus the previous view from the people's part of the church through the arch where the wall was built and on through the monks choir and presbytery to the high altar at the far end was completely blocked by a wall of masonry.

Once the new octagonal tower was finished, the monks moved their bells into it, but in order to prevent the parishioners having their own set of bells in their own tower the monks walled up the entrance. This so enraged the parishioners that serious disturbances took place resulting in cases being brought before the Court of Assize. Twenty-four of the town's principal inhabitants (including the four churchwardens) were bound over to keep the peace in sums of £100 each and two further securities of £20 each. These are the equivalent of about £35,000 and £7,000 respectively in today's money, giving some idea of the severity of the incidents.

The early years of the fifteenth century continued to see numerous incidents, some ending in court proceedings and frequently concerning bells and the hanging of them to call the faithful to prayer. After false starts and periods of inaction, permission was granted for the north-west tower to be removed, the present north aisle built and the present west tower to be built to house the town's bells.

As has been seen the abbots of St Albans had regarded themselves as being in absolute control of the Priory. In 1446 one of the monks of St Albans, Stephen London, was appointed archdeacon and, making use of his new status seems to have told the abbot what he thought of him. The result, perhaps to get rid of Stephen, was that he was appointed Prior of Wymondham.

This was a bad mistake on the part of the abbot, since Stephen turned out to be a well-liked prior both by the town and the patron as well as the monks themselves. The abbot then tried to remove Stephen who promptly retaliated by having the patron, Sir Andrew Ogard, send a petition to King Henry VI. The petition cited the original foundation document and reminded the king that it conferred upon him the power whenever he and the patron so chose to raise the status of the priory to that of an abbey. The past catalogue of disputes was also recited and the king gave his permission. Pope Nicholas V in 1448 ordered the change of status, appointed Stephen London to be the first abbot and ordered that all future abbots should be chosen from the monks unless with the general agreement of the patron and the monks. Thus independence from St Albans was ensured.

For nearly a hundred years things seem to have been calm and peaceful until the Dissolution of the monasteries was ordered by Henry VIII.

The Manors of Wymondham

For most of its history, Wymondham was split into various manors, but originally, as has already been stated, at the time of the Norman invasion, the whole of Wymondham was held by Stigand, the Archbishop of Canterbury. Most of this landholding eventually passed to William d'Albini and formed one large manor. The remainder was acquired by another great lord, William de Warenne.

In 1107 William d'Albini split his manor by founding the priory in Wymondham and endowing it with one third of his great manor (as well as other pieces of land elsewhere). The other two-thirds remained as one large manor until it was split up in the early thirteenth century.

Manors were landholdings, originally held by feudal tenure, which could be inherited or sold. They included the demesne, which was the land farmed by the lord of the manor himself, while the rest of the land was held by tenants who either paid rent or provided labour services. The latter (villeins) were tied to the manor and were also required to pay the lord at times, including inheritance and marriage. These services declined after the Black Death (1349) and villein tenure evolved into copyhold tenure, with money rents, which was only abolished in 1924.

The manors also had the right to hold courts. The court baron recorded the transfer of copyhold lands on sale or inheritance. The courts leet were more important: they dealt with petty law and order issues, administration of communal agriculture and also recorded all the adult males who were required to be members of groups of about ten men, responsible for each others behaviour (view of frankpledge). The courts were usually administered by the steward of the manor because the lord of the manor frequently lived elsewhere, owning manors in different places.

Although these manors may have originally been distinct parts of Wymondham, by the post-mediaeval period the landholdings seem to have become mixed, so records show the open fields contained strips belonging to several manors.

Three of the manors were attached to religious houses. The main one was the Abbot's Manor, this being the third of the Wymondham great manor that William d'Albini donated to the new priory to provide income. The prior/abbot was entitled to hold his own court leet. William d'Albini also donated a second manor in Wymondham to the prior, that being the manor later known as Downham Hall Manor. This was the separate hamlet in Domesday Book, called Hidichethorp. The prior built a country seat or house of retirement there called Downham Lodge.

The third manor held by a religious house was that of Chossells (or Choseleys). This was another gift from William d'Albini, this time given to the church of St Lazarus of Jerusalem at Burton Lazars near Melton Mowbray in Leicestershire. This manor had a court leet with sole jurisdiction over its own tenants.

7. The ruins of Westwade Chapel on the bridge over the Westwade stream as recorded by Thomas Martin, a Thetford antiquary, in 1722. Built by the Wymondham Priory, it was dedicated to The Holy Cross. Offerings were collected from travellers, most probably in return for using the bridge.

At the Dissolution of the monasteries in the sixteenth century all three of these manors passed into secular hands. The Abbot's Manor initially went to the Earl of Surrey until he was executed. It then reverted to the Crown, being held by both Queen Mary and Queen Elizabeth, hence its new name of Manor of the Queen. It continued in royal possession thereafter. Before the Dissolution the last abbot had assigned Downham Hall Manor to John Flowerdew of Hethersett. The manor then passed through various hands, including the Buxton family in 1623, and eventually was acquired by the Wodehouses of Kimberley.

Choseleys Manor was initially given to John Dudley by Henry VIII, as part of the Burton Lazars estate. Dudley sold it to William Kett in 1545, but Kett was later executed due to his involvement in Kett's Rebellion and the manor went to the Corporation of Norwich on behalf of the Great Hospital there.

All the other manors in Wymondham (apart from one mentioned below) arose from the breakup of the d'Albini great manor in the early thirteenth century.

Apart from the abbey holdings, the two major manors were Grishaugh and

Cromwells. They were both entitled to hold courts leet. Between them they owned both the Great and Little Parks and Grishaugh Wood. In addition, the market and fairs came under the jurisdiction of Grishaugh. They separately passed through various hands until acquired by the Hobarts of Blickling in the sixteenth and early seventeenth centuries respectively. The Hobarts also acquired a third Wymondham manor, Rustens, at around the same time.

These three manors were therefore combined by the early seventeenth century. As the major landholder and administrator of the market, the Hobart family had influence in the town although living elsewhere. In the 1770s the Hon. Henry Hobart was involved in the planning of the building of the new House of Industry at Wicklewood and at the time of parliamentary enclosure in 1806 the manors were held by Revd Henry Charles Hobart.

Other manors in Wymondham from the d'Albini's great manor were Gunvills, Stalworthy, Burfield Hall, Nothes, Brockdish and Wadcars. Stalworthy, Burfield Hall and Nothes were separate during the mediaeval period, but eventually joined together as one manor, which was later held by the Burroughes family, including Randall Burroughes at the end of the eighteenth century.

The one manor that did not arise from the d'Albini's great manor was Stanfield Hall. This was the land held by William de Warenne at the time of Domesday. This manor again passed through various hands over the years.

These details show that there was little stability in the ownership of some of the manors through the years, although the changes probably had little effect on the peasants working in the fields: they still had to provide rent or labour services. The biggest change was at the time of the Dissolution of the monasteries when the three manors held by religious houses passed into secular ownership (Manor of the Queen, Downham Hall Manor and Choseleys Manor).

The Black Death and the Peasants' Revolt

Plague arrived in Dorset on 23rd June 1348 with some Gascon sailors and proceeded to make its way rapidly throughout the length and breadth of the country. The population of the country had almost trebled in the years since the Conquest, but before the end of 1349 nearly half the population had died. In Europe as a whole 25 million people died in just five years between 1347 and 1352 – a third of the population.

Opinions today seem divided as to the reasons for the spread of the disease, but the most commonly held belief is that it was spread by rat fleas and then by infection from those who had it. The connection with rats was not recognised at the time.

This visitation, however, was not the end of the plague. It came and went in waves over the following centuries. The last recorded outbreak was in East Suffolk between 1905 and 1911. The effect of the Black Death in Wymondham is not known, but it seems unlikely that the town escaped. Its inhabitants certainly suffered in later outbreaks.

This destruction of such a vast proportion of the labour force, not surprisingly, enabled the survivors to improve their pay rates despite government measures to peg these at pre-Black Death levels. However, loss of revenue and continuing wars needed further funding and in 1377 a Poll Tax of 4d a head was declared. This was increased to one shilling a head in 1380 and led in the following year to the Peasants' Revolt.

Beginning in Kent and with Wat Tyler as their leader, an army of rebels marched on London causing death and destruction but the rising ended after only a month with Tyler's death. There was at the same time considerable activity in East Anglia. In Norfolk there seem to have been several bands roaming the county and attacking and laying waste property and crops, notably of religious houses such as St Benet's Abbey and Carrow Priory. One band was led by John Bettes of Wymondham who at his later trial was charged along with thirteen others, many from neighbouring villages such as Wicklewood. Curiously Bettes seems to have been more fortunate than many others and was acquitted.

It should not be thought that the uprising known as the 'Peasants' Revolt' consisted only of peasants. The Poll Tax fell on all equally despite their rank or wealth and many felt the iniquity of this. Sir Roger Bacon of Baconsthorpe was persuaded to join as were four other knights from the county.

The rising in Norfolk, led by Geoffrey Litster from Felmingham, escalated to a gathering on Mousehold which then occupied Norwich and its castle. Henry le Despenser, Bishop of Norwich, having been with troops quelling uprisings in other parts of East Anglia, returned and with little difficulty routed the rebels at a final battle near North Walsham on 26 June 1381.

Meanwhile the Black Death continued to rage with a further serious outbreak in 1390. The larger cities were the worst hit and Norwich was not spared. Sir John Paston writing from Hampshire to his brother back at home in Norfolk in 1471 refers to *'great death in Norwich'* and *'the most universal death that ever I wist in England'*. Subsequent outbreaks in 1563 even caused Elizabeth I to move her court from London to Windsor and the Great Plague in London in 1665 really only came to an end with the Great Fire in September 1666 and the onset of winter which reduced the rat population, and thus their fleas, and the spread of the bacillus. 1632 seems to have been a bad year for Wymondham with the inhabitants of Norwich raising money for the Wymondham poor.

Religious Guilds

Guilds had existed in Anglo-Saxon times, but throughout the Middle Ages and up until the Dissolution they grew in popularity, prestige and wealth. Many people felt the desire to have masses said for the souls of the departed, (including, of course, themselves) when they passed on. Becoming a member of a guild was a convenient and reasonably certain way to achieve this. Since each guild retained a chantry priest or chaplain to say masses and ensure proper burials for its members.

As the fourteenth and fifteenth centuries progressed, however, the guilds became much more than this. From the simple desire to ensure the saying of masses and shorten the time that the soul spent in purgatory, they evolved into a mixture of a social club and a friendly society. Different guilds evolved in different ways, some into trade-regulating bodies for specific crafts, others into the religious guilds of which at the Reformation there were known to be twelve in Wymondham.

By the time of the Dissolution, guilds were providing for candles to be kept permanently alight before the altar in the guild's chantry or chapel, sometimes in an independent building but most frequently found within the parish church. It also arranged for the proper burial of its members, organised services to commemorate the festival of their patron saint, held an annual feast (a social event and fund-raiser for lamp oil), provided loans to members and grants for sick members.

Membership of the guilds seems to have been open to both men and women and to all levels of society. Strict rules were passed and breaking them usually meant a fine either in money or in pounds of candlewax. Many of the rules centered on encouraging the members to attend church but others were of a more secular nature. The Guild of the Nativity of the Blessed Virgin, for example, even provided what lawyers would today call 'Alternative Dispute Resolution'. At a time when resorting to the Courts was an uncertain and expensive business, the guild required its members to submit their dispute to the judgement of the senior officers of the guild to see if it could be settled without going to court. This was enforced by a fine of four pounds of wax if they failed to do so.

As the popularity of the guilds increased and their size with them, so too did their administration. Most guilds had an alderman but there could also be a dean, a steward, a crier, beadles, purveyors, a *pincerna* or butler or standard bearer. The election of the officers was an important annual event and attendance, as usual, was commanded on pain of a fine.

The muniment room at the Abbey contains books of account for a number of guilds including the Guilds of St John the Baptist, All Saints, the Light of Our Lady, The Trinity and the Nativity of the Blessed Virgin. A copy of the Rules of the last is also to be found there.

Fairs and Markets

There were several royal charters for fairs and markets issued to Wymondham during the medieval period. As with the majority of such charters issued throughout the country, they were probably acquired by payment to the royal exchequer, this being a useful form of royal fundraising.

The first charter for a three-day annual fair, to be held in September, was granted by King Stephen in 1135 to the monks of Wymondham, giving the priory a useful source of income. This charter was renewed by Henry II.

In 1204 King John granted a charter for a fair to William, Earl of Arundel, also to be held in September. This raises a query: did the priory therefore lose this source of income? At the same time King John issued the first known charter for a market in Wymondham, to be held on Fridays. This was also issued to the Earl of Arundel. In 1207 the day was changed to Tuesdays. There may well have been an unofficial market earlier: the charter from William d'Albini founding the priory in 1107 mentioned the 'market-court'.

In 1440 new charters were issued for both the fair and the market by King Henry VI. The charter established a fair to be held in May. This time, both charters were issued to the men and inhabitants of Wymondham. It appears that the local people had taken the initiative. However, the market was administered by the Manor of Grishaugh until the twentieth century.

By the post-mediaeval period, the market was held on Fridays and the fairs were held three times a year, in February, May and September.

Manorial Life after the Black Death

The Black Death is believed to have killed about one third of the population when it reached England in 1348–49. It is not known what happened in Wymondham at that time, but presumably there was a large death toll here as elsewhere. However, one result of this catastrophic event was the gradual change in status of the manorial tenants, due to the labour shortages caused by the death of many of the population. An example of these changes can be seen in the records of Grishaugh Manor, which still exist (held by Norfolk Record Office).

Until 1370 Grishaugh Manor was run on normal medieval lines with the direct administration of the manor locally by the steward of the lord of the manor and most labour being provided by labour services of the unfree manorial tenants.

In the mid-1300s the manor buildings (probably on the site of Park Farm) consisted of a hall, chapel and chamber, kitchen, treasury, barns and stables. There was also a mill and a dovecote. The manor lands were spread through the parish of Wymondham, although the manor buildings lay in the large hunting park (which was part of the manor) to the south of the town. Farming was mixed, with arable lands growing wheat and barley, meadows and pasture for stock, plus Grishaugh Wood (in the park) providing another resource, wood.

The lord of the manor's demesne was land reserved for his own use, as distinct from land held by tenants. In Wymondham the Grishaugh demesne was administered directly for the lord's benefit until around 1370. Until that date he received a sizeable income from the fixed rents of the tenants, income from the sale of wheat and barley, also from stock, especially sheep, wool, wood and also from fines issued in the manorial courts. Some workers were employed, such as ploughmen, but other tasks such as hoeing, threshing and winnowing were amongst the labour tasks required from unfree tenants. The lord's profit in 1362–63 was nearly £100.

The change in the lordship of the manor with the inheritance by John Clifton in 1368 led to the demesne being leased to various tenants around 1370 and the labour services expected from the unfree tenants were commuted to cash payments. Similar changes were being implemented throughout England during this period. Direct administration of the demesnes of many manors was being found to be uneconomic due to the labour shortages caused by the Black Death, so it became more profitable to lease the land out for fixed money rents. It also passed the problem of finding and keeping labourers to the lessees.

As a result of this devolution, the Grishaugh manorial records no longer showed the details of cereal and stock sales and daily agricultural tasks seen in the accounts during the period of direct demesne cultivation because these were now the responsibility of the lessees. Instead, the demesne was leased out in small parcels for a number of years. From this time on, the income of the lord was from these leases as well as from the payments due from the commutation of labour services. In addition, he still received the rents from the other tenants as well as the income from the manorial courts and from the sale of wood.

Throughout this period, this manor, as well as many others, was run on behalf of the lord by a group of hired officials who visited Wymondham when necessary. These men were all gentlemen and frequently lawyers, who were employed to offer advice as well as administering the lord's estates. They included the receiver (i.e. of monies collected), the auditor, the supervisor (of all the estates), the steward and substeward. The latter two held the manorial courts including the leet court and served as chief legal counsel to the lord.

Locally there were two types of officials. First, those hired by the lord and only responsible to him were the bailiff, parker, and the bailiff and clerk of the market court. The other type were local men who formed part of the customary government and were elected by their fellow tenants at the manor court. These officials included the reeve, the collector, the four haywards (for each of the four divisions) and the custodians of the woods and of the fields. These men all owed certain responsibilities both to the lord and to their fellow tenants.

Much of the material used here comes from the Grishaugh bailiff's and haywards' accounts. Each of the four divisions in Wymondham (Norton, Wattlefield, Suton and Silfield) had its own hayward and also provided its own jury to the manorial courts.

The accounts show that the bailiff was responsible for the collection of rents for the meadows and pasture lands and for the harvesting and sale of wood. He was also responsible for the repairs of any structures owned by the lord including palings, fencing, hedges and folds. In addition, he received the monies collected by the haywards and paid any expenses when necessary. He was paid a salary of 60s 8d per year (sometimes more).

The duties of the parker (who also received a salary similar to the bailiff's) are unclear from the available records. The bailiff of the market collected the rent of the market stalls and fines from the market court. He served both Grishaugh and Cromwells Manors as they held the market jointly.

The other officials were elected at the Michaelmas manor court each year. Those eligible for election would have to be tenants of certain defined tenements. In East Anglia rents and services were tied directly to the holdings themselves, called tenements (i.e. a block of land). This was unlike other parts of the country where status was personal and tied to the person, i.e. either a free or unfree villein. In East Anglia the status of a tenement, rather than its holder(s), determined its obligations. Manorial offices such as reeve or hayward passed in rotation among selected tenements regardless of personal status. By the fifteenth century, many tenements had been subdivided into several holdings and all the tenants of the subdivided tenement were liable for the attached duties as a group.

In Grishaugh Manor, thirteen tenements shared in rotation the office of reeve, thirteen the collector, thirteen the Norton hayward, twelve the Wattlefield hayward, eleven the Silfield hayward, eleven the Suton hayward, five the custodian of the woods and five the custodian of the fields. Therefore, a total of eighty-three tenements carried with them some sort of responsibility for offices, along with the rents due.

Once these changes took place, the four haywards were the most important officials of Grishaugh Manor. After direct demesne administration ceased, they were no longer responsible for any animals or crops of the lord and they became rent collectors. They collected the rents from the tenements plus the sums owed from the leased demesne lands, and also the sums due for the commuted labour services and other customary payments. They also had to attend the manorial and leet courts, ensuring the appearance of witnesses etc. required to attend. In addition, they distrained the chattels of those owing rents or fines.

The normal payment the haywards received for this work was very low, only being a rent allowance of 4s each for Norton and Wattlefield, and 3s for Suton and Silfield. However, the position was not onerous and gave a man some standing in the community. Sometimes the position was held by the major holder of the elected tenement, sometimes by a paid replacement.

The offices of custodian of the woods and of the fields did continue to exist but were rarely mentioned in the accounts outside the annual election. Both were responsible for preventing animals straying, either in the woodland or in the fields as appropriate. These officers were subordinate to the Norton hayward.

After the leasing of the demesne, the manor buildings were gradually sold, leaving only the lodge in the park to be used as an administrative centre. It is not clear where the manorial courts were held. The treasury was sold in 1374–75 for 13s 4d, the hall in 1379–80 for £13 6s 8d, the chapel and kitchen for £8. The mill was last mentioned in the accounts in 1380–81 and the dovecote only until the end of the fourteenth century. No manor house was needed because New Buckenham Castle, the seat of the manorial family, was only about ten miles away.

The park itself continued to be managed by the bailiff. It held woodland, pasture and meadows (these two let to tenants) as well as providing hunting. Earlier accounts mention pannage (the right to graze pigs), a rabbit warren and a mill pond. However, the rabbit warren was never let for more than 6s 8d per year and no rabbits were ever mentioned in the accounts. By the mid-fifteenth century, it had disappeared from the accounts, replaced by a close called Conyler which was let for 7s per year, probably as pasture.

The wood was farmed systematically by coppicing and cropping in rotation. It provided oak for pales for the park fence, oak bark to be sold for tanning, and underwood sold as firewood, in bundles of faggots. When the widowed Lady Clifton was living in Kimberley (the park was part of her jointure) delivery of firewood to her necessitated large scale carting operations. For example, 60 carters were needed to carry 4,000 faggots in 1416–17 and 45 men in 1417–18.

The park boundary (*see Fig. 4 for an aerial view*) continued to be maintained, including repairs to the palings, hedges and ditches. Offences appearing in the manorial and leet courts included breaking into the park and taking animals, taking wood, and damaging hay and wood. For example, Simon Wellyng took a heifer in 1402, Simon Longyerd a cow in 1434.

Again in 1402, William Blyth was fined 6s 8d for taking a deer without licence.

8. The Green Dragon, Church Street, built in the late fifteenth century.

Oaks were stolen in 1447 and 1498, and underwood in 1449. Stray animals were impounded and owners fined: horses were the most frequent strays seized, followed by cattle, pigs and sheep.

Religion played an important part in medieval life and even cropped up in the manorial courts when various men in the fifteenth century were fined for unjustly accusing their fellows in the church court, but the nature of these accusations is unknown.

However, Richard King of Wymondham was convicted in the Norwich heresy trials in 1429. He confessed to denying transubstantiation and the use of images in a church. He was flogged around the church on three successive Sundays, carrying a wax candle weighing one pound, and every week for a year had to hold a torch costing two shillings as the host was elevated in the Mass.

Various Grishaugh haywards were more conventional in their religious beliefs, leaving wills containing pious bequests common at the time. For example, John

Langford left 12d to the altar of the parish church, 15s for the building of the new bell tower, 13s 4d for repairs to the Abbey and 40s to various religious houses in Norwich.

The Textile Industry

Rearing sheep for their wool and turning this into fabric has been carried on in East Anglia since Roman times. It was not until after the Conquest that it began to become an industry. Most of Norfolk has a fertile soil which lends itself far more to arable farming than to sheep running. The Norfolk breeds of sheep produced short wiry wool of an inferior quality to that produced in other parts of the country so that as a wool-producing area Norfolk did not excel.

By the thirteenth century, however, the situation was changing. Norfolk, with its east coast ports, had long enjoyed trade with Holland, Belgium and the other countries bordering the North Sea and the Baltic. Thus when life became difficult for the population of those countries ravaged by war and flooding, it was quite natural for them to look for new homes in East Anglia. The Flemings had begun arriving in small numbers ever since the eleventh century and many settled in and around Norwich, which would have inevitably included Wymondham. They brought with them their skills in weaving and were largely instrumental in establishing and then enlarging the trade and taking the area to the forefront of the worsted weaving industry. Their presence in the area meant that it was worth importing the raw wool from other parts of the country that produced sheep with long soft fleeces.

The prosperity of the wool weaving industry in Norwich and other parts of the country grew and by a Royal Statute of Edward III in 1353 a formal organization was set up in a handful of towns, of which Norwich was one, with a 'Mayor of the Staple' and a court to control the trade. The increasing control of the trade meant that Wymondham would have been compelled to operate through the Norwich staple along with all the other outlying areas. By this period Norwich was one of the wealthiest towns in the land and was empowered by Royal Charter to make many of its own laws.

Numerous different types of cloth were being woven in the area from the cheapest fustian and bombazine to the finest camlet described by William Paston in the Paston Letters as being *almost like silk*. Cloth for commercial sale would have and separate and have not been matted together as in woollens. Perhaps the easiest way of distinguishing them is that worsted can be unpicked from the edge whereas woollen fibres are so matted together that unpicking is impossible.

The weaving trade was extremely labour intensive with numerous different skills being needed from the first treatment of the raw wool through to the dispatch of the

9. An early sixteenth-century survival: a former butcher's shop in Market Street with a roll-moulded bressumer.

finished cloth. The majority of Wymondham households would have been involved in some way. Practically every unmarried woman or spinster spent some of her time spinning, in the earlier days of the trade with a distaff and later, with the need for a more even product required by worsted, using a spinning wheel.

Conclusion

It has been argued that the fifteenth century was the peak of Wymondham's importance and prosperity. The Abbey obtained its independence from St Albans in 1448 and the long-standing disputes between the monks and the townspeople were settled. This prosperity was reflected in changes made to the church with an enlargement of the north aisle which was fitted with the fashionable Perpendicular windows. In addition, the great new west tower was started and considerable changes were made to Becket's Chapel (in use as a guild chapel). In the secular domain the feudal system was changing, the textile industry was becoming well-established and the revised market and fair charters were obtained in 1440 from Henry VI.

CHAPTER THREE

The Sixteenth Century

The Reformation and the dissolution of Wymondham Abbey

The historical developments which took place in the mid-sixteenth century have been described as the greatest upheaval before *c*.1760 when urbanisation and industrialisation began. Not least among these were the changes which took place in religious doctrine and the government of the church in England from 1536 onwards. Those with the most impact in Wymondham were probably the changes in the form and practice of worship in the parish church which preceded and accompanied the dissolution of the Abbey and the religious guilds. At the same time, the Tudor monarchs were vigorously promoting the parish (the word 'township' was also taken to refer to the whole parish, not just the town proper) as its agent of secular government. The extent to which this eroded the influence of the manors in local affairs will be considered later.

Wymondham Abbey on the eve of its dissolution

Traditionally, the picture painted of the Dissolution of the monasteries has been one of harsh intervention by Henry VIII in the affairs of 850 defenceless spiritual power houses, of their despoliation to fill royal coffers and bind to the Crown gentry who bought or were given monastic land. The implication, too, is that a major source of help to the community, and especially to the poor, was demolished. The prejudiced reports of Thomas Cromwell's visitors painted a picture of the monasteries as dens of iniquity where monks and nuns lived lives of luxury and moral depravity, the negation of their original purpose. Charges of inefficiency were made by landowners completing the catalogue of reasons for liberating monastic property into lay hands.

We can judge how accurately these charges applied to Wymondham Abbey from the reports of bishop's visitations and in particular that of 1514. This was conducted by Richard Nix, Bishop of Norwich 1501–1535, a strict conservative and opponent of religious reformers and the royal divorce. The twelve monks and their abbot were questioned individually and encouraged to report on each other. What emerged was a general laxity in the conduct of the monks who were not kept under the firm discipline of their Rule, much internal bickering and pettiness, and some implied sexual contact with women. Ignorance of the names of his monks meant that the abbot, Thomas Chamberlen, lacked interest in leading his community. He did not prevent monks from writing to the bishop without permission, prohibit the wearing of secular dress or the possession of private property. The prior, William Bury, was universally described by the brothers as a dangerous lunatic given to violent attacks on others. He attended daytime services very infrequently and, in part due to his failure to apply control, the night offices were not observed. In general he was an object of derision and fear.

The most obvious charge against the brothers was that they led near secular, insufficiently spiritual lives and were no longer serving the local community. Accusations of improper relations with married women and the girls from 'Le Dearie' were freely made, especially against the chamberlain, John Blome. The duty to help poor children and provide a schoolmaster had been neglected. Land had been let by the previous abbot to two local men for their lifetime without the brothers' consent. Finally, the bishop imposed the most extraordinarily mild injunctions to the effect that laymen should not be given any office within the monastery unless they swore to keep its secrets. The prior was to be removed from his office, but remained in the monastery where he became precentor by 1520 and resumed as prior by 1526. Therefore, it is likely that few local people regretted the passing of the Act for the Dissolution of the Lesser Monasteries in 1536.

The Dissolution

Relations between the monastery and the parishioners had been fraught in the past. Indeed, the nave of the priory had only been secured by the parish as its church in 1411 and the parish bells finally hung in the new west tower by $c.1500$. However, when in 1538 Henry VIII sent John Flowerdew, a serjeant-at-law living at Stanfield Hall, to supervise the pulling down of monastic buildings, local feelings were aroused once more. The parishioners paid the king for the abbey steeple and bells, the south aisle and other monastic buildings and materials, only to find that Flowerdew intervened in a high-handed fashion. The parishioners had bought 17 flodder (1 fodder = $c.1$ ton) and 31 feet of sheet lead from the dismantled buildings, but Flowerdew would not hand it all over. He melted down a considerable amount and poured it into a hole in the churchyard where it stayed until its rediscovery in the mid-nineteenth century. He also pulled down and sold much of the stone of the south aisle, south transept, Lady Chapel and founder's wall. Such was the anger generated against Flowerdew by his actions that it contributed to the outbreak of Kett's Rebellion in 1549.

Meanwhile, the abbot and monks were pensioned off. Abbot Elisha Ferrers was given a most generous pension of £60 13s. 4d. and the monks were found work as parish clergy.

The religious guilds

Religious guilds were a feature of life in towns in medieval and pre-Reformation times (*see p. 21 above*). Wymondham possessed twelve guilds by 1524. The oldest, St Thomas the Martyr, dated from 1187. The majority were established in the fifteenth century, while the Guild of the Holy Spirit was founded as late as

10. Wymondham Abbey from the Abbey Meadows, showing the chapter-house arch and the shell of the central lantern tower.

1524.

The guilds received bequests in cash and land, not least for the maintenance of their guildhalls, the centre for much of their social activities. There were at least eight halls in the late medieval period, four of them in the town proper.

11. The sole surviving religious guildhouse: hall of the All Saints Guild, 29-31 Damgate Street (now a private house).

The government of Henry VIII took supreme control of the Church in England. Secular authority achieved a paramount position in its control and the rising tide of Protestantism increasingly influenced changes in the nature of the church as an institution and in its doctrine. The Injunctions of 1538, published by Thomas Cromwell with the authority and co-operation of Thomas Cranmer, continued the attack against medieval superstition begun in 1536. In particular, they launched a wholesale attack on idolatry, demanding that *'For avoiding that most detestable offence of idolatry'* images were to be removed and the clergy were to *'suffer from henceforth no candles, tapers, or images of wax to be set before any images or picture'*. In future the only lights to be permitted would be on the rood loft, before the sacrament on the altar and to illuminate the sepulchre. Thus the essential purpose of religious guilds was removed. But the guilds did not disappear overnight in Wymondham: the evidence of wills suggests that even after 1535 seven guilds received gifts, four are known to have rendered accounts between 1540 and 1545 and new entrants were being received into St John's Guild in the 1540s, the last being in 1547.

The final blow was struck by Edward VI who secured a Chantries Act in 1547 dissolving 2,374 chantries and chapels where priests said masses for the souls of the departed. Included in it was the provision that all the possessions of the guilds would pass to the King from Easter 1548. In this way Wymondham lost bodies that had been making an important contribution, albeit informally, to the worship and social life of the parish. The guilds had provided a way for groups of people to express their parochial piety in their own idiosyncratic ways, to achieve identity within rather than separate from the parish community. The main form of lay religious activity had been destroyed. There were immediate protests from the burgesses of King's Lynn and Coventry at the removal of the guilds and increasingly at the loss of schools occasioned by the Dissolution of the monasteries. In 1561 Elizabeth I granted to the township of Wymondham the lands and houses called the 'Townlands' formerly held by the Guild of St Thomas. These were entrusted to a group of thirteen named feoffees (trustees) who were to employ the income from these properties to maintain a free grammar school and for other charitable purposes such as the relief of the poor.

Kett's Rebellion

Robert Kett – a yeoman farmer with a conscience

> *By bearing a confident countenance in all his actions, the vulgars* (common people) *took him to be both valiant and wise, and a fit man to be their commander. Life of Edward VI,* Sir John Hayward

Kett's fame rests largely on the last five months of his life from July to December 1549, in particular the six weeks he spent at his camp on Mousehold Heath, near Norwich. Before this he was little known outside Wymondham. The stirring and dramatic events of those weeks have been described many times and can be studied elsewhere. Here we are concerned with the man and the town in which he spent his entire life, until the events of the summer of 1549 ended it so tragically.

Evidence about Kett's life is fragmentary, but what does survive, when considered in the light of contemporary events, allows a tentative picture of this complex and elusive man, born in 1492, the fourth son of Thomas and Margery Kett. He married Alice Appleyard of Braconash and they had four sons. In due course, he became a prominent and influential figure in the town.

While the cause may have produced the man in the Norfolk Rising (usually known as Kett's Rebellion), it was the man who made the cause. So it is perhaps useful to discuss the factors which helped to make the man who is inseparably linked with the 1549 rebellion.

First, the town where he grew up and made his way in life must have played a vital part in this process. The Wymondham which Kett came to know and care for as much as anyone, was a community of some 1500 souls dominated by the Abbey.

12. Early sixteenth-century houses: 19-21 Cock Street

During the Middle Ages, the town had become an important religious centre with the Abbey, Becket's Chapel and Becket's Well, whose water was believed to have sacred and healing powers, acting as a magnet for pilgrims. Even after the Dissolution 1536–1540, this medieval religious legacy remained important. The annual fair held to commemorate Thomas Becket, a popular saint in Wymondham, reflected this and this religious background must have had an effect on Kett, a factor to which we will return.

Wymondham was also a flourishing market centre, whose position on the road from Norwich to London, contributed to its prosperity. The main occupation was farming but there was cloth making, a thriving wood turning industry and also some trade in leather. Some early writings refer to Kett as the 'Wymondham Tanner'.

Genetic traits and family roots of course also contributed significantly to the making of Kett's character. The Kett family has been described as *'an ancient and flourishing'* one. The Ketts were of Danish origin with roots traceable to pre-Conquest times; their vitality, vigour and openness to new ideas were characteristic of the Norsemen. These qualities were displayed by various members of the family who showed an independent spirit and became freemen in early Norman times; they recovered their status and wealth and became substantial local landowners.

During the fifteenth century, the Ketts were enterprising landowners and public figures in Wymondham, testimony to the family's flair for leadership. Richard Kett, Robert's great grandfather (died 1476), was an alderman of a guild with land on the outer parts of the parish and properties in the town itself, including in Damgate; he was also a founder member of the Guild of the Nativity of the Blessed Virgin. John Kett, Robert's great uncle (died 1512), was the principal landowner in Wymondham according to Blomefield. He was also a butcher and a member of the Guilds of St Peter and St Thomas and in 1481 was elected town reeve. He bequeathed legacies to the high altar, for church repairs and to the Guild of St Thomas as well as to relatives. Robert's father, Thomas, who died in 1536, farmed some twenty acres in Browick and also had land in Forncett together with a number of properties near the Abbey and in Middleton Street. He, too, was a butcher and also an active member of the Guild of Brotherhood of Our Lady's Light. It is clear then that the Kett family was prospering and steadily increasing its influence in the town, a trend which Robert continued as did his older brother William, with whom he seems to have been particularly close.

Kett's character was also moulded by religion. Like his ancestors, he was closely associated with the Abbey. He was probably educated by the monks and had close links with the last abbot, even naming one of his sons, Loy, after him. As a young man he was a tenant of the Abbey and after its dissolution acquired some monastic land himself. He was also a server in the abbey church and church warden with responsibility for certain altar vessels and candles. His brother, William, was similarly involved. Kett's deep affection for the Abbey and the parish church became clearly evident at the time of the Dissolution when he took a leading part in the efforts to keep parts of the abbey church for the town.

Kett was also very involved with the religious guilds in the town whose corporate and social life included feasts, pageants and helping the poor. He was a member of the Guilds of St Thomas and St George and also involved with the Watch and Play Society, a group which organised pageants and mystery plays. It is significant that the Lady Chapel which had its own guild was one of those parts of the former monastery saved for the town by Kett and others after its dissolution. But it was perhaps the teachings of the guilds and their daily life, which played the most important part in influencing Kett. They gave him valuable experience in organisation with their emphasis on self-help which became vital elements in the orderly camp on Mousehold. Their religious nature may well explain, too, the strong moral ethos at the camp, where daily religious services were held. Among the famous Requests drawn up by the rebels and sent to the King was, *we pray that all bond men be made free, for God made all free with his precious bloodshedding'*. It could be argued that this was a central idea rather than a symbolic one and further evidence of the religious roots of Kett's thinking, representing an attempt to confront contemporary problems with a radical reshaping of social and economic rights based on the teachings of the Gospel.

A fourth factor in Kett's make-up was economic. He came from a family of farmers and it is no surprise that he continued in that tradition. A rising yeoman farmer during the 1520s and 1530s, he steadily acquired land in the parish. After the Dissolution when much land was changing hands, he made further gains and, by 1549, he was a substantial landowner in the area with some 50 acres to his name. These included properties in Middleton and Town Green and a house in the shadow of the Abbey, possibly near his tan pits. At the inquest into his affairs after the rebellion, it was recorded that his land consisted of the Manor of Wymondham, lands belonging to the hospital of Burton Lazars in Leicestershire, two tenements in Cavick near the marl-pits, including pasture and arable and finally Gunvills Manor. Through a combination of astuteness and hard work, Kett had achieved a secure and solid position in the community and there is every reason to assume that this process would have continued but for the events of 1549. He was a tanner as well as a landowner and his tan pits were probably in the Tiffey meadow by the Abbey.

Kett's assumption of a central role in the events of 1549 is in part a result of his relationship with John Flowerdew, a rising lawyer with land at Hethersett. Flowerdew was appointed as Crown agent to oversee the demolition of the monastery in Wymondham. The two men did not seem to have been on good terms before the upheaval of the Dissolution; they had been rivals for land in the Browick area in the 1520s and early 1530s and a scribbled note survives in the Abbey muniment room, referring to a debt Flowerdew owed to the Kett brothers which he had to settle, before he could take up another piece of land.

However, it was the events of the Dissolution in 1536–40 which brought the rivalry between the two men into sharper focus. Flowerdew acted in a high-handed way by lining his own pockets with the spoils of the Abbey such as lead and stone. This triggered a campaign by Kett and other townsmen, who petitioned King Henry VIII to buy back parts of the Abbey for the town. Kett played a leading role in this campaign to save the parish church and its fabric from someone perceived as an ambitious lawyer, aspiring to the squirearchy. Kett had a deep affection for the church and as a result of the campaign, Henry VIII granted the town lead, bells, timber and glass and also parts of the Abbey building, such as the steeple, vestry, south transept, the choir, St Margaret's chapel and the Lady Chapel. The parishioners were also allowed to keep Becket's Chapel which had probably been used by the guilds for the performance of mystery plays.

The bad feeling between Kett and Flowerdew was further inflamed in 1549 at the time of the annual fair to commemorate Thomas Becket. The fair was the catalyst for Kett's emergence as a leader of the commons against the oppressive and monopolistic rule of the Norfolk gentry, who had been abusing their powers by enclosing much of the common land around Wymondham and throughout the county, causing widespread hostility. A large crowd had come to the town to enjoy the pageantry, mystery plays and street entertainment. However, the general discontent among the poor, now gathered in large numbers in the town where drink was plentiful, may well have given them the confidence to voice their grievances more loudly. Some two weeks earlier there was anti-enclosure rioting at Attleborough, where local landlords had enclosed part of the commons.

At some point during the festivities in Wymondham, a group took it upon themselves to go to Morley and pull down the fences erected by the lord of the manor, John Hobart. Later that day, perhaps spurred on by this example, others set off for Hethersett, where Flowerdew, already unpopular because of his role in the dissolution, had enclosed part of the extensive Wymondham common. However, Flowerdew seems to have anticipated trouble and when the unruly mob arrived intent on pulling down his fences, he was ready with a bribe of 40 pence which he used to divert the rioters back to Wymondham, pointing out that Kett had also been enclosing common land, possibly near the Fairland.

There now occurred the turning point in the events of that long weekend. When confronted by the angry rioters, Kett offered to join them, saying, according to the Chroniclers, *'Whatever lands I have enclosed shall be made common again unto ye and all men and my own hand shall first perform it'*. He then began to pull up his own fences. It was an extraordinary moment. Kett had recognised that enclosure was a social wrong and despite the disadvantage to himself, he took the first decisive steps to join the rioters believing that their cause was a just one and it was the right thing for him to do. It is not too fanciful to suggest that this decision, based on a concern for the plight of others, had its roots in his experiences in the guilds which were such a formative influence on his character. After his own fences had been uprooted, the group returned to Hethersett where, after *'many sharp words'* (Holinshed), Flowerdew's fences were also pulled down.

But Kett was not merely offering support to the cause but to be its champion. Within twenty-four hours, he offered to lead the poor in *'defence of their common liberty'*, adding that he was *'ready to do whatever, not only to repress but to subdue the power of the great men'*. He went on, *'Never shall I be found wanting where your good is concerned. You shall have me if you will, not only as a companion but as a captain, and in the doing of so great a work before us, as a general standard bearer and chief'*. It was an offer which was readily accepted, no doubt because of his reputation in the town as a forthright and sincere man. His clarion call reveals a man driven by conscience, confident in his own ability to lead a movement of protest against economic and social injustice.

Next day, Kett led his followers on a great protest march to Norwich, probably stopping at 'Kett's Oak' outside the town to make another rousing speech. It proved to be a fateful decision, but Kett seems to have now made up his mind. In the next few weeks he transformed a disparate collection of the lesser orders of society, numbering some 15,000, into a coherent social force for reform against corruption in the county, appealing to the King for *'justice and good governance'*.

By the mid-1540s, Kett had become a respected and respectable pillar of the Wymondham community. His personal qualities made him a major player in the economic, religious and civic life of the town. He was accustomed to taking the initiative and asserting himself and it is no surprise that he did so decisively in 1549, for a cause which he deemed worthy of his personal support.

13. Kett's Oak between Wymondham and Hethersett at which Kett is thought to have addressed his followers in July 1549 before advancing to Norwich.

In the end Kett and his motley army were defeated near Norwich. He himself was hanged from Norwich Castle and his brother William suffered the same fate from the tower of Wymondham parish church.

Kett remains a complex and elusive figure whose contradictions make him a continuing challenge for historians. The debate about his motives will continue, but his decision to lead a protest from Kett's Oak, seemed to be based on moral foundations and his personal impact on the events of the next six weeks, made an indelible impact on Norfolk and English history. However, in the short term, the effect of the unsuccessful rebellion on the town's inhabitants may well have been dispiriting.

The churchwardens and religious change

By the mid-sixteenth century, the four churchwardens had major ecclesiastical and civil duties under the law within the smallest unit of royal government, the parish. The burdens placed upon these unpaid officials by the Crown steadily increased under the Tudors, not least because of the major changes in religious doctrine and the governance of the church which took place during the Protestant Reformation. At the same time the basic functions of the churchwardens made constant demands upon them. They were responsible for maintaining the fabric of the church, providing for services and upholding doctrinal and moral standards. They could make bye-laws on all matters of public concern. A welter of other activities filled

14. Parke's butcher's shop, Market Street, built in the sixteenth century. This once had an oriel window attached to the broad horizontal beam at first floor level.

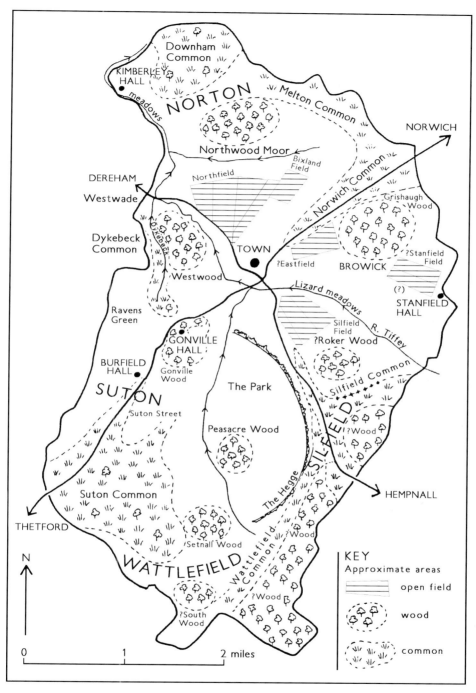

15. A sketch map of the parish of Wymondham c.1600, showing the approximate areas of the commons, common fields and woods.

41

their year in office and these are well represented in their accounts which in the sixteenth century survive for only eleven years between 1544 and 1561.

Repair of the parish church occupied much of the churchwardens' time, mainly because of the devastation wrought to the south aisle by Flowerdew and its protracted rebuilding, but also because the period covered by their accounts coincides with major upheavals in doctrine brought about by the Protestant Reformation and Henry VIII's break with Rome. The churchwardens' accounts for 1550–52 reflect the considerable work load involved in profiting from the building materials of the monks' parts of the Abbey: lead, glass and bells from the lantern, broken stone from the south aisle all brought in money. The following extract indicates the scale of the sales operation.

> *Memorandum that the hoolle inhabitantes of the township of Wymondham dyd bargayn and selle unto oon Thomas Cowper of Ipyswiche merchannte 6 bellys & 1 foder of lede for the som of – £62 5s*

£58 of the above money was used immediately to purchase a house and land formerly belonging to the Guild of St Thomas rather than the repair of the south aisle. The high altar was taken down and replaced by a communion table in the same period. Sir John Robsart and Lady Knyvett, both from leading Norfolk families, took into their safekeeping two expensive proscribed vestments, a *'cope of cloth atyssue'* and a *'vestment of black vellett with a white saten crosse'* respectively. Other vestments had to be paraded before the royal commissioners at Hingham and Norwich before their disposal in 1552–54. Then Catholic Mary came to the throne in 1553 and the whole process was reversed. The high altar was restored. The figures of Christ, the Virgin Mary and St John were re-erected on the rood screen and in 1557–58 the holy water stoop was set up again. The rollercoaster ride continued when Elizabeth became Queen. Some features of the Henrician church were retained with a slightly more moderate interpretation of Edwardian doctrine, However, the Injunctions of 1559 were *'for the suppression of superstition'* and *'to plant true religion'* and so the high altar was removed once more in favour of a table, new liturgical works introduced, the second Edwardian Prayer Book reimposed and by 1560–61 images and the whole rood including the screen taken down. A printed calendar of the Henrician saints' days was officially displayed in the church.

A mere listing of physical changes can only tell part of the story of religious upheaval. Certainly the tone of the Elizabethan church settlement was more moderate than Edward VI's but what actually happened in Wymondham was probably different in subtle ways from the government's demands. One clue is provided by an inventory of *'all the churche ornaments remaynynge in the vestry'* taken by the churchwardens on 1st December 1564. This amounted to 37 items which included four vestments that would have been illegal under Edward and a number of altar cloths and hangings which belonged to the catholic order of things. However, the prevailing spirit in Wymondham was to be increasingly Puritan as the sixteenth century gave way to the seventeenth. By 1584–85 John More, the Puritan 'Apostle of Norwich', was preaching in Wymondham which indicates the religious tendency of the town.

CHAPTER FOUR

The Seventeenth Century

The government of Wymondham

The sources of authority in the parish or township

Wymondham was the fourth largest Norfolk town by population in 1600 with about 2,250 inhabitants and yet it did not secure a borough charter. There were three main sources of authority in the parish: the lords of the manors, the church and authority outside the township in the county and London.

The manors

The manorial system continued to function in much the same manner in the sixteenth and seventeenth centuries as it had done in medieval centuries: it acted as the means by which agriculture was organised co-operatively in the areas of the open fields not yet enclosed, the commons and township meadow land.

Two types of manorial court were held: the court baron and the court leet. Courts baron were held in each manor every three weeks and dealt with changes in the ownership of copyhold land belonging to the manor which was let out to tenants who held a copy of the entry in the rolls of the court. By its terms, tenants paid a modest annual rent for use of the land, but a relatively heavier fine for entry to a holding obtained by purchase or inheritance. This court, run by the lord's steward, would settle minor disputes relating to the manor and its tenants. Judgement would be made by 'suitors', those who owed a duty to attend and take part in its proceedings. Failure to attend without good reason would lead to a fine.

Courts leet were only held in the Manor of Grishaugh but served the whole township. Thus they were much weightier affairs than courts-baron. An original purpose of a court leet was to hold the view of frankpledge, an account of the number of persons over the age of eleven who resided within the jurisdiction of the leet for a year and a day. The court sat twice a year, as originally laid down in Magna Carta, normally within a month after Easter and within a month after Michaelmas (29 September). The lord of the manor or his steward acted as judge and had the authority to enquire into all cases of injury, trespass, debt and other actions involving claims over 40 shillings up to but not including High Treason. The power to punish in the more serious cases lay with the Judges of Assize to whom they would be referred. The court spent much of its time regulating local agriculture. It also passed bye-laws, as in 1635 when a bye-law was passed in the presence of 220 people to restrict incomers to the town who might become a burden on the poor rates.

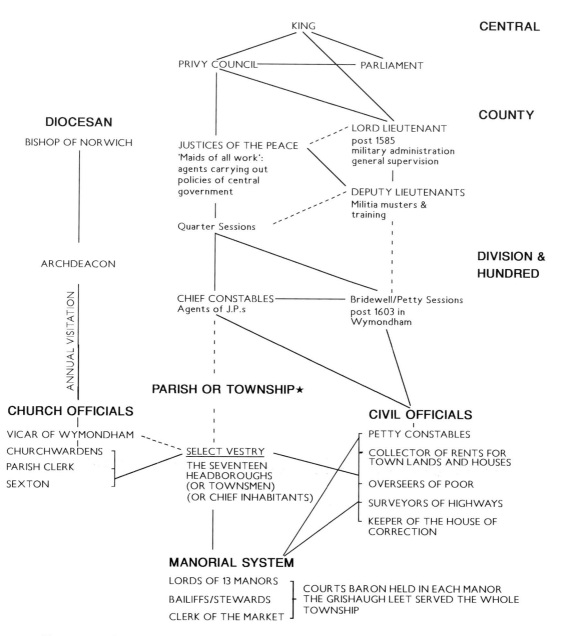

CENTRAL

KING

PRIVY COUNCIL ——————— PARLIAMENT

COUNTY

DIOCESAN

BISHOP OF NORWICH

LORD LIEUTENANT
post 1585
military administration
general supervision

JUSTICES OF THE PEACE
'Maids of all work':
agents carrying out
policies of central
government

DEPUTY LIEUTENANTS
Militia musters &
training

Quarter Sessions

DIVISION &
HUNDRED

ARCHDEACON

ANNUAL VISITATION

CHIEF CONSTABLES
Agents of J.P.s

Bridewell/Petty Sessions
post 1603 in
Wymondham

PARISH OR TOWNSHIP★

CHURCH OFFICIALS

VICAR OF WYMONDHAM
CHURCHWARDENS
PARISH CLERK
SEXTON

SELECT VESTRY
THE SEVENTEEN
HEADBOROUGHS
(OR TOWNSMEN)
(OR CHIEF INHABITANTS)

CIVIL OFFICIALS

PETTY CONSTABLES

COLLECTOR OF RENTS FOR
TOWN LANDS AND HOUSES

OVERSEERS OF POOR

SURVEYORS OF HIGHWAYS

KEEPER OF THE HOUSE OF
CORRECTION

MANORIAL SYSTEM

LORDS OF 13 MANORS

BAILIFFS/STEWARDS

CLERK OF THE MARKET

COURTS BARON HELD IN EACH MANOR
THE GRISHAUGH LEET SERVED THE WHOLE
TOWNSHIP

★ The precise relationship between the components of Wymondham's 'government' is uncertain.
People often served on several different bodies within the township and the work of those
bodies tended to overlap. Thus the reality was less clear-cut than this diagram may suggest.

16. Diagram showing how Wymondham was governed in the seventeenth century.

The church

The church also played a major role in the 'governance' of Wymondham. From as early as the fourteenth century, meetings of the vicar, churchwardens and leading parishioners had taken place on Sundays after the morning service. Because this meeting was often held in the vestry, the people who met there came to be known as a 'vestry'. The 'principal parochial personage' in the parish was the parson – the vicar in Wymondham's case, as the rectory passed to the Crown and thence to the Bishop of Ely after the dissolution of Wymondham Abbey – but of the vicars we know relatively little. Many of their duties are not mentioned in surviving documents. Apart from routine spiritual ones, they were required to attend whippings at the market cross; they supervised public confessions demanded of offenders by county magistrates and the penances imposed by church courts.

Of the churchwardens we hear much more, first through their surviving accounts and then from the volumes of the Town Book (surviving from *c.*1585 onwards), an invaluable source for Wymondham history under the Tudors and Stuarts. These contain the annual accounts kept by the vestry after the feoffees, who were responsible for using income from the town lands to run the school, merged with the membership of the existing vestry. Until the 1560s, the vestry was dominated by four unpaid churchwardens who were elected annually at Easter at a vestry meeting. The churchwardens' powers originated in the parish as an ecclesiastical organisation. They administered common property and made bye-laws on matters of public concern. They could raise a rate for the relief of the poor and any other purpose which they felt the inhabitants would accept. They were responsible for the maintenance of the fabric of the church, control of the paid officials – the parish clerk and sexton – and presentation of a report to the archdeacon's visitational court which came to Wymondham annually. This report was based on a questionnaire and covered crimes relating to the church, clergy and parishioners.

In addition the Tudors chose to make the parish the smallest unit of civil government and imposed an ever-increasing burden of statutory duties upon parishes generally and churchwardens in particular. From this body there developed a form of select vestry, known in Wymondham in the early seventeenth century as 'The Seventeen'. The first surviving membership list of this select vestry, dated 1604, is to be found in the Town Book and it is clear that its members often served until they died. In an open vestry they would have been annually elected. While the details are not entirely clear, the most likely explanation is that the 'headboroughs', as the vestry members were often called, were not elected, but formed a ruling elite, a form of town council. It was based in part on ownership of certain ancient manorial tenements, a degree of nepotism and trust from the populace at large that they would carry out their duties in the interests of all. There was much overlap between membership of the vestry and the manorial courts, especially the Grishaugh court leet. The members included some of the wealthiest and best educated inhabitants of Wymondham, lawyers, merchants and yeomen.

Authority outside the parish

One reason why Wymondham failed to secure borough status may be the absence of any major personages living within the parish boundaries. Important gentry lived just outside the bounds of the parish – the Wodehouses at Kimberley, the Knyvetts at Ashwellthorpe – or well beyond it in the case of the Hobarts at Blickling, the Lords of the Manors of Grishaugh, Cromwells and Rustens, controllers of the market and the holders of the leet for the whole of the township. Local JPs were required by statute to maintain law and order and to attend to matters concerning roads, bridges, poor relief, binding apprentices and granting begging licences. From time to time they intervened in Wymondham's affairs and liked to be seen doing their duty by local people as well as fulfilling their statutory obligations. In turn, local magistrates could be prompted by privy councillors in London to attend to Wymondham's affairs. An example of this kind of intervention occurred in 1622 when complaints reached the Privy Council from the *'minister, churchwardens, overseers and other inhabitants of Wymondham'* that the income from the town lands was not being properly employed and the keeper of the new bridewell was too impoverished to do his job effectively.

Wymondham's government in the seventeenth century varied in its efficiency and the variety of work undertaken on behalf of the community. What seems clear is that the decline in the manorial system which was a marked feature of many other areas from the sixteenth century onwards does not appear to have occurred in Wymondham until a later time. Rather it was a case that the part played by manors stood still while the work of the vestry advanced until about 1660. By that time, much of the structure established to deal with government-inspired responsibilities had achieved an independence of the vestry, at least in financial terms. Depending on the accounts in the Town Book for much of our information about Wymondham after 1600, it is clear that the 1650s form a kind of watershed. Before that decade the headboroughs appear deeply immersed in the work of the churchwardens, maintaining the town's properties on which its income depended, defending the interests of local inhabitants before the law and, as feoffees, showing a compassionate face to the world. After the Civil Wars there is an increasing concentration on the work of the feoffees of the charity, upon relieving the poor and maintaining the free grammar school. Entries in the town's accounts become formulaic with seemingly endless details of small sums and items of clothing given to the poor. It is as though the Puritan conscience at work increasingly among parishioners had brought a new seriousness to the conduct of the town's business.

The Great Fire of 1615

On the morning of Sunday 11 June 1615, while many of Wymondham's inhabitants were in church, a fire quickly took hold in two areas of the town. Fire was an ever-present danger in towns like Wymondham where thatch and timber construction were still the norm. What made this conflagration unusual was that it was started deliberately not accidentally. By the time it had been brought under control 327 inhabitants had lost goods and/or houses. Over a quarter of the town's population had lost its housing and upwards of a third suffered direct loss of housing and/or goods. Including dependents, approximately 620 people may have been directly affected or about 55% of those living in the town proper. These claims are listed in *The Booke of the Losses by the fire 11th June 1615*, but the document does not allow us to count the total number of houses lost and it remains silent on the precise location of the houses.

The exact starting point of the fire is not known and the sources are in some disagreement about whether the fire was started in a stable or the eaves of a house. Two sources are agreed that the fire was the result of deliberate arson by three gypsies, William and John Flodder, Ellen Pendleton, John's 'pretended' wife, and

The Woefull and Lamentable wast and spoile done by a suddaine Fire at S. Edmonds-bury Aprill 1608.
Printed for *Henrie Gosson,* and are to be solde in Paternoster rowe, at the *Signe of the Sunne* 1608
17. The limitations of fire-fighting methods in the early seventeenth century.

The Araignment of Iohn Flodder and his wife,

at Norwidge, with the wife of one Bix, for burning the towne of Windham in Norfolke, upon the ix day of June last 1615. Where two of them are now executed, and the third reprived upon further confession.

18. Heading and woodcuts from the first page of the ballad concerning the arsonists who set fire to Wymondham in 1615. Published by John Trundle, London (1616).

a local accomplice called Margaret Bix, alias Elvyn. It seems that they had intended to set fire to Norwich but their lodging keeper suspecting them to be *'unruly and disordered persons'* locked them in at night. As a result they decided to move to Wymondham and burn that town down instead. According to Bix's confession, she only met Ellen Pendleton three days before the fire and being promised a better life and a pardon from the Pope agreed to help the conspirators.

The motives of the arsonists are not totally clear. A northern Catholic plot to assassinate James I was feared and in the course of infiltrating the group of conspirators, the report of a government agent suggested that some people were blaming the burning of Wymondham on Catholics. Just ten years after the Gunpowder 'Treason' it was not surprising that there was some prejudice against Catholics. Further evidence inclines to this view. Ellen Pendleton claimed under examination that *'wandering companies'* were being employed by Lord Stanley to burn down towns with inhabitants of a strong Puritan persuasion. A contemporary broadsheet ballad, *The Araignement of John Flodder and his wife*, described John

Flodder as *'a self-wild Papist, of a stubborne heart'* and tends to confirm that Bix was *'will'd to put her hope at last, to have a Pardone from the Pope'*. However, the ballad suggests that the conspirators were habitual beggars, travellers who sustained themselves by seeking relief in each town they visited while indulging in other criminal activities at the same time. It may be that the burning of Wymondham was an act of spite against a town that had not provided the level of relief they had expected. Certainly local people had a reputation for being charitable to those in dire need, but equally for being averse to supporting 'foreign' counterfeit beggars.

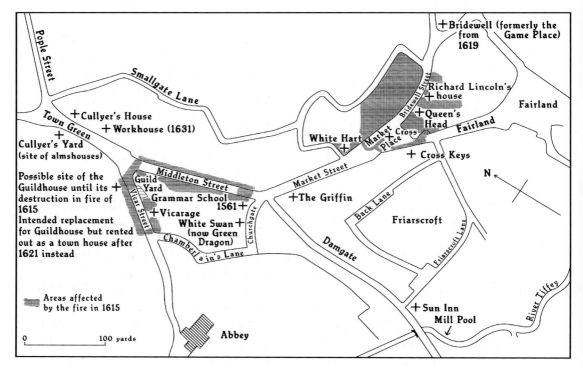

19. Sketch-map of Wymondham showing the current estimate of areas affected by the fire in 1615.

Contemporary evidence suggests that the fire took hold very quickly and that by the time people came out of church it was very difficult to stop. While we have evidence for the number who suffered loss by the fire, we do not have any documentary accounts of the spread of the fire. That the fire was disastrous is not in doubt but it was not the catastrophe suggested by the ballad; later claims, based on the ballad, asserted that the losses amounted to £40,000 when the true figure was £14,944 19s 0d. We know that the market cross, the schoolhouse, the vicarage and the guildhouse were destroyed.

These were buildings of importance to the town: the market cross was a rectangular building probably with an open ground floor to provide cover for traders and an upper storey with a room for the use of the market court and clerk of the market. The schoolhouse was a timber-framed building which together with Becket's Chapel provided space for teaching and accommodation for boarders. The vicarage must have been an impressive building as it boasted a gatehouse with a chamber above it. The guildhouse was used by the select vestry as a kind of town hall. It was here that the vestry met to draw up its accounts for the year and that meetings of the headboroughs or townsmen took place. Much money had been lavished on this building in the decade before the fire.

A study of the buildings that have survived suggests that much of the town centre escaped but also that the fire was probably started in two different areas: in the Market Place destroying the market cross and in Vicar Street destroying the vicarage and the guildhouse. The Green Dragon, then probably called the White Swan, survived, as did Becket's Chapel. The marking on the timbers of the inn is not due to scorching. And so it is difficult to see how the fire spread from Vicar Street to the cross, or vice-versa, and yet missed the White Swan. The map on page 50 shows a current estimate of the areas affected by the fire. Thus in the absence of specific documentary evidence it is necessary to work out the course and geographical extent of the fire by studying the surviving buildings and trying to estimate their ages. It is very difficult to arrive at a building's date within a decade either side of 1615. It is more realistic to aim to distinguish between houses built in the fifteenth and sixteenth centuries and those which are of the early seventeenth century. Apart from decorative features applied to houses when first built, what helps to distinguish post-fire buildings is that in Wymondham smaller, lighter timbers were used post 1615 than in the sixteenth or the later fifteenth centuries. By the 1620s vertical timbers (studs) are more widely spaced and the joists used in jetties stand on edge while earlier ones lie flat on their broad sides. Where original chimneys have survived, they grew simpler in the seventeenth century: the intricate shaping of individual flues in the sixteenth century, as in No. 66 Damgate Street, gives way to multiple flues contained within a plain square or rectangular stack, as in Bridewell Street.

The evidence of surviving buildings tends to support the view that the fire spread eastwards from the White Hart (now Heart of Wymondham) up the north side of Market Street and so down Bridewell Street and Fairland Street. Examples of pre-fire buildings are fairly plentiful: No. 3 Market Street, Parkes the butcher's shop, show the heavy timbering of the sixteenth century. The houses of the south side of Market Street clearly escaped the fire as the deep roll moulding of the bressumer of No. 12, formerly a butcher's shop, shows. Conversely Bridewell Street displays a marked seventeenth-century character. Here we have a dated example, the so-called 'Manor House', built by Richard Lincoln, a wool chapman, as an inscription in a downstairs room testifies. In the other area, Vicar Street and Middleton Street appear to have been affected by the fire. Whilst this is conjectural, the fact that the present buildings in those two streets are of the seventeenth and later centuries tends to support such a conclusion.

An emergency on the scale which faced Wymondham in 1615 demanded the intervention by leading gentry from the county. This meant Sir Henry Hobart of Blickling, Lord Chief Justice of the Common Pleas and in Wymondham Lord of the Manor of Grishaugh, with its control of the market, Cromwells and Rustens. He had an obligation as senior lord of the manor and a leading figure on both the county and national stage to be seen to be involved in the relief of the town. It was he and his fellow JPs who organised the gathering of claims for losses in the fire by five gentlemen from the Wymondham area; only one, Thomas Weld, was an inhabitant of Wymondham itself.

After a ten month delay *The Booke of the Losses* was complete and received the approval of Sir Henry and his gentry friends. Much of the data in this list is difficult to analyse beyond the simplest level. Claims were made for a 'house', 'houses' and 'goods'. In all it is possible to identify 22 individual houses, the claims for which averaged £27 19s. This was a fairly high average but it is difficult to say whether this reflects exaggerated valuations or the high quality or large size of houses. Excluding the township's claim for a loss in 'public' buildings and town houses of £1,000, the average loss per claimant amounted to £42 15s 6d. The claims varied in size from £700 for houses and goods by the wealthy grocer, Stephen Kett, to the loss of goods amounting to 5s by Anne Tomblesom. A total of 35 claims were for sums in excess of £100. The highest claim for goods was for a substantial £140 by Robert Hempson. Women feature prominently among the claimants with 112 entries, 34% of the total. 49 (15%) of these are widows, mostly with claims for goods as the majority of them would have been dependent upon a relative for their accommodation. A handful of these women had been independent before the fire like Anne Gedney who claimed for goods worth £120, a sizeable sum, but not too surprising because, after the death of her husband John, she had continued to run his lucrative business as an innkeeper.

Money needed to be raised to provide some relief for those who had suffered loss. Quite separate from other people was Edward Agas, the vicar of Wymondham. His living was poorly endowed given the wealth of the parish. All that was left to him from the tithe income, after both great and small tithes had been granted to the Bishop of Ely, was half the small tithes or about £25 per annum, while the tithe farmers, acting indirectly for the bishop, raised between £500 and £600 annually. Thus it was that an individual appeal for contributions to relieve the distress of Edward Agas was made to the clergy of Norfolk by John Jegon, the Bishop of Norwich, on 29 July, 1615:

...The most lamentable casualtie and infynite losses by the fier in the towne of Wymondham in June last past, as it was to the utter undoing of most inhabitants there, soe to Mr Edward Agas Vycar there irrevocable, whoe lost all whatsoever he had even howse, howshold stuffe, bookes, and notes of all his studies in tymes past, save onely the cloathes of his back and the Bible in his hand in the tyme of the sermon ...

But for the majority, the normal procedure in such a disaster was to secure a major appeal by royal mandate under letters patent to all church and secular authorities in a prescribed list of places to organise the collection of alms in relief of those who had suffered in the fire. No copy of this document is known to have survived but we know from the ballad the names of the eight Wymondham men entrusted with visiting the parishes in London and Westminster, Middlesex, Essex, Kent, Hertford, Surrey, Sussex, Canterbury, Rochester, the Cinque Ports and the city of Chester to collect their contributions. The whole procedure under the terms of the royal 'brief' took six years. The brief raised £2,171 8s 5d of which £2,003 8s 5d was distributed among the claimants other than the township and the vicar. These payments were made by means of five 'distributions' and one additional set of payments by warrant. It was a very long time to wait for payments which averaged £6 13s 6d or nearly one seventh of the amount originally requested, especially for the poorest claimants. It is impossible to categorise the groups which did relatively well, or badly, or failed completely. Elizabeth Kett, widow of Valentine Kett received 94% of her claim or £12 10s out of £13 6s 8d. Some received nothing: Dr Thomas Talbot had asked for £500 and, at the very bottom of the pile, Anne Tomblesom received not a penny of her 5s claim for burnt goods.

The rebuilding

Surviving evidence provides no more than an impression of how well and how quickly Wymondham recovered from the fire. Even though local JPs met in each of the two years before the fire to consider what could be done to relieve the poor and the collector for the poor, Arthur Earle, was holding back £42 2s of poor relief money by 1616, very few payments were recorded in the Town Book in support of the poor in the critical years immediately after 1615. By contrast certain major buildings were replaced at an early stage.

In 1615 *'certaine oakes* [were] *bought of Fynderne to the use of the towne for the rebuildinge of the schoole'* and in 1615–16 2,924 boards were sawn from these oak stocks for the same purpose. Overall £33 9s 2d were spent, including £30 repaid to Philip Cullyer which he had spent *'towardes the building of the schoolehowse'*. The other important building replaced was the Market Cross. At the urging of Sir Henry Hobart, lord of the Manor of Grishaugh who carried responsibility for the market, the site of the old rectangular market cross was levelled and with another loan from Cullyer of £25 7s the new cross was completed between 1617 and 1618.

20. *Bridewell Street which was rebuilt immediately after the fire. 'The Manor House', first owned by Richard Lincoln, is the first building on the left.*

It seems probable that the market, a weekly trading event of considerable commercial importance to the town, was functioning immediately after the fire, for William Burrell was paid expenses of 4s as clerk of the market in 1616–17. Yet this rebuilding was not without its drama. In his absence, Sir Henry Hobart's 'officers' prepared to erect shops upon Market Hill. Wymondham people responded angrily and promptly drew up a petition to Sir Henry complaining that the shops would be *'an exceedinge great blemishe both to the Crosse & market place'* leaving *'no standinge for cattell, nor convenyent place for people to walke in'* and further that the matter was *'so grevous to diverse of your Lordshipps tennanntes ther about dwellinge, whose estates were ruinated by the fyer & nowe to reedifye ther howses have layd ther best meanes upon them'* that they *'do wyshe they had never built at all'*. The lack of any reference to this episode in the years following suggests that the petition succeeded.

It is uncertain whether the guildhouse was rebuilt. In 1620–21 the town paid 5s 2d to *'the Princes Surveyor about a platt* [plan] *for the guild howse'*. However, accounts for the next six years are missing and its is not until 1627, when the next volume of the Town Book was begun, that we learn that the headboroughs were continuing to meet in the schoolhouse. No further mention of the guildhouse is made. Meanwhile the vicarage had been rebuilt for Edward Agas in Vicar Street.

Private houses were not always replaced with as much speed as 'public' ones.

LIVE·WELL·AND·DIE·NEVER ·DIE·WELL·AND·LIVE·EVER·

RICHARDVS·LYNCOLNE ⊞ANNODOMINNI⊞1616

21. Proof of early post-fire rebuilding in Bridewell Street: an inscription from a beam in 'The Manor House'.

Documents suggest that the town had plentiful supplies of trees which were carefully managed to provide a variety of different types and scantlings of timber for building work. Tedds, a carefully tended area of pasture land belonging to the town, regularly produced sizeable quantities of timber. And yet, while the houses in Bridewell Street seem to have been rebuilt very promptly, as the inscription dated 1616 in Richard Lincoln's house suggests, there were clearly fire damaged sites left empty for some years. A survey of 1621 stated that Esaye Freeman had six tenements not yet rebuilt; Doctor Woodhouse, Christopher Browne, Thomas Agas junior, Doctor Wells, Humfry Burrell, Stephen Kett, Stephen Wyseman and John Parsley each had one tenement in like condition. The 'guildhall' is also listed as not reconstructed. Some properties were still not rebuilt in the mid-1630s as is revealed in a byelaw passed at a meeting of the Grishaugh leet on 1 August 1635 which sought to limit the erection of new houses in Wymondham. It specifically excluded any site where a dwelling stood on 11 June 1615 and *'was wasted and consumed by the fyer'*. Further it anticipated that it might take a further ten years for some of the rebuilding to take place.

Recovery from the effects of the fire seems to have taken until the outbreak of the Civil War in 1642. The entries in the Town Book in the period 1615–21 give little hint that the town was in a crisis: major buildings which reflected local pride were rapidly reconstructed and dignitaries who visited the town were generously entertained. However, while there were many prosperous inhabitants, like the headboroughs, who appear to have taken fire losses in their stride, it was for many a time of distress. A letter of 1622 from the minister, churchwardens and other inhabitants of Wymondham to two Justices of Assize reveals that twelve people were on the point of starvation and about 400 living in poverty. To make matters worse the town lands were being misemployed by Arthur Earl, a corrupt collector,

22. The Market Cross built between 1617 and 1618 to replace its rectangular predecessor which was destroyed in the fire of 1615.

and the poor law was not being properly enforced. The two decades following the fire were times of considerable economic and social suffering: a slump in the cloth trade after 1618, a depression (1621–23), plague (1625), a stop in trade (1629), crop failure and plague (1630–31) and a return of plague in 1636. During the 1631 outbreak the death rate trebled and the people of Norwich collected £103 5s 7d for relief work and cautiously locked their gates to prevent visitors to the Wymondham fair bringing the pestilence into the city. Such difficult circumstances must have slowed the processes of rebuilding and recovery for many. But lessons were learned: the fire of 1615 was the last major one to affect the town although there were minor outbreaks. In 1616–17 a group of poor men were paid for putting out a fire at Damgate Bridge and in January 1640/1 other poor men received 10s for quenching a fire in Back Lane near Damgate Street.

Contrasting lifestyles

Early seventeenth-century Wymondham society was divided into rather loosely defined classes below the ranks of the true aristocracy.

The gentry

In practice the wealthier members of rural society and urban professionals were regarded as gentry by local people. This group in order of their status embraced baronets (a hereditary title created by James I for purchase in 1611), knights (self-evident from their title), esquires (possessed a coat of arms) and gentlemen (in theory entitled to a coat of arms but in practice a more loosely defined status implying that they did not work with their hands). With the exception of Dr Thomas Talbot, the leading local gentry all lived just outside the township. For example:

Sir Anthony Drury (c.1580–1638), Sheriff of Norfolk (1618), Deputy Lieutenant, MP, JP, of Besthorpe Hall

Sir Thomas Knyvett (c.1596–1658), JP, of Ashwellthorpe Hall

Dr Thomas Talbot (c.1561–c.1628), Judge in the Vice-Admiral's Court in London, JP, of Gonville Hall

Sir Thomas Wodehouse (1585–1658), second baronet, Sheriff of Norfolk (1625), Deputy Lieutenant, MP, JP, of Kimberley Hall

These men were engaged in county politics and local government as well as having friends at Court or on the Privy Council in London. Therefore, apart from their large houses and estates in the countryside, they might own or rent town houses in Norwich and London. They intervened in the town's affairs as local JPs or when prompted to do so by higher authority.

Gentlemen

Just below this level were a few professional men, including lawyers, doctors of physic, the grammar school master and the vicar, who lived within the town, for example,

Thomas Weld, gentleman, lawyer (c.1598–1664), JP, of Cavick House

Mr Edward Agas, Vicar of Wymondham 1607–29, B.A., Corpus Christi College, Cambridge

Mr Thomas Leverington junior, Master of Wymondham Grammar School 1603–06, headborough 1604

Like his father before him, Thomas Weld played a prominent role in the town's affairs, frequently being called upon to act in legal disputes affecting the town and being responsible as a local JP for swearing in the first civil register, the parish clerk, Thomas King, in 1653. Weld was fortunate to become a JP It was his value as a loyal parliamentarian with legal training which perhaps explains his appearance on the bench in 1650 rather than his social status which hitherto would have been insufficient. What these men shared in common, and indeed with the leading local gentry, was a university education at one of the Cambridge colleges. The links between them were quite strong. They met at quarter sessions, through their roles in the government of Wymondham, through marriage and the farming of land. In their own ways they shared the task of running the township's affairs but from different directions: the leading gentry by intervention from outside, the professionals from within but in close co-operation with the middle stratum of Wymondham society, wealthy yeomen and merchants.

Yeomen and merchants

Just below the status of gentlemen, yet often more than equal in objective terms with them, came a significant group of prosperous yeomen. 'Yeoman' was originally a term denoting the ownership of freehold property, but was essentially a mark of status rather than describing an economic role. Such men were Philip Cullyer and wealthy merchants like Thomas Crane. Quite apart from their entrepreneurial success, they were involved in the heart of Wymondham's government as headboroughs and often acted out of a desire to serve their community in a variety of ways.

Husbandmen and tradesmen

Husbandmen were tenant farmers with smaller incomes than most, but not all, of those who styled themselves 'yeoman', e.g. John Randall. Tradesmen covered a very wide variety of occupations. The most prosperous were those who ran their own businesses, such as the brewer, Thomas Woodcock, and the butcher, Thomas Moore. The relatively poor craftsman were dependent on a master, such as were probably the linen weaver, Thomas Cole, or the woolchapman, Richard Lincoln, a travelling salesman. Richard was sufficiently well off in 1616 to replace his house after the fire of 1615. He claimed that the house he had lost was worth £30 and received £5 towards its replacement from payments under the royal brief. However, by the time he died, his movable possessions were worth only £16 2s 2d, of which £2 7s 6d were bad debts.

Labourers

Of these there is little record because inventories were not required of those whose moveable goods were worth less than £5. Among 164 wills and 46 inventories – a majority of the survivals for Wymondham in the seventeenth century when only 25–33% of adult males made wills – only two wills are specifically of labourers. We have to glean what information we can from indirect sources such as wage rate assessments. Many would be virtually indistinguishable from the poor into whose ranks they often fell.

The poor

At times of economic distress as many as a fifth of Wymondham's population would have been dependent on relief provided by the parish poor rate and the town lands' charity. In a letter written in November 1622 it is reported that ' . . . *there are at this instant some Sabboath dayes twelve or more prayed for in the Church and readie to perish for want of foode, the number of the severall persons of the poore being in the same towne about 400'*. And this was in a parish of about 2,250 people. Many of the poor were orphans, widows and the aged sick, but, where labourers were dependent on seasonal work, they could cycle in and out of extreme poverty. Alice Ludkin represents the very poorest. Her inventory was valued at 19s 2d of which 16s was in cash together with a petticoat worth 2s, a kettle 8d and a bedstead 6d.

Evidence from inventories

An Act of Parliament of 1529 required executors of wills to produce a detailed list and valuation of the 'goods, chattels and cattle' of the deceased where these were worth more than £5. An inventory was drawn up by three or four friends and neighbours of the testator who were thought competent to value his goods. While there are limitations to the quality of evidence they provide – the contents of all rooms may not have been examined, the appraisers' valuations could be inaccurate and goods might have been disposed of before death – inventories give us some

Inventory category	Sir Anthony Drury	Thomas Crane draper	Philip Cullyer yeoman	Thomas Moore butcher	John Randall husbandman	Richard Lincoln woolchapman	Alice Ludkin poor
Date	1638	1603	1625	1629	1636	1634	1592
Total value	£3908 2s	£578 9s	£204 15s 4d	£71 7s 2d	£27 13s 6d	£16 2s 2d	19s 2d
Clothes	£60	£9	£5	£2	£1 5s	10s	2s
Cash	£238 10s	-	£1 19s	£3 10s	£6	12s	16s
Plate	£450	£3 6s 8d	£16 10s	-	5s	-	-
Good debts	£1500	£468	£15 19s	£14	£5 10s	£2	-
Bad debts	£700	-	£20	-	£5 10s	£2 7s 6d	-
Rooms	31	8	8	3	3	3	1
Rooms with beds	19	5	4	2	2	1	1
Linen	£100	£12 7s 8d	£4 12s	£3	10s	-	-
Outhouses	8	6	5	1	-	1	-
Books	-	3	36	2	4	-	-
Virginals	1	1	1	-	1	-	-
Animals	cowes, horses, sheep, poultry, pigs	-	mare, colt, nag	6 horses	colt	mare, foal	-
Crops	corn, wheat, barley, hay, oats, cheese	-	wheat, maslin, malt, barley, rye	wheat, peas, barley, vetches	-	wheat, barley	-

23. The table above is based on data from probate inventories. It indicates the range of wealth in Wymondham, from the rich to the poor.

basis for comparing the lifestyles of the different classes in society. A glaring example of a near certain omission is the lack of any reference to books in Sir Anthony Drury's inventory, for he was a Cambridge graduate and deeply involved in public affairs.

A detailed study of one individual may provide an insight into life in Wymondham more generally in the Jacobean period.

Philip Cullyer (*c*.1558–1625), yeoman, a good servant of Wymondham

What distinguished Wymondham from the other large Norfolk towns was that its affairs were run by a group of prosperous lawyers, merchants and yeomen, as only one of the leading local gentry lived in the township. What marked out these men was their willingness and ability to serve their local community. But while some were also keen to profit from this work, others devoted themselves unselfishly to the interests of the town and its inhabitants. Philip Cullyer was just such a man and through an examination of his life we can learn a little about the lifestyle of a headborough in the late sixteenth and early seventeenth centuries.

Philip Cullyer, one of the more prosperous yeomen in Wymondham, belonged to an extensive family that had lived in the town since about 1390. Like his father and grandfather before him, Philip steadily increased his wealth by adding to the land and property he had inherited. His will refers to five separate items of houses and land in Wymondham, as well as 12 acres of copyhold land in the Manor of Swanton Abbott, 4 acres of copyhold land and some further houses in Aytonfield Manor and two acres of land *'inclosed more or lesse lyeinge nexte Norwood Comon which is mortgaged unto me by Nicholas Baxter for thirtie poundes'*. His immediate bequests in money amounted to £100, including £16 p.a. for life; a series of further bequests conditional upon reaching a certain age totalled an additional £55. The impression created is of a man of comfortable means.

While probate inventories cannot always be taken as an accurate guide to a yeoman's wealth, in part because land and real property might be otherwise recorded, the impression formed from Cullyer's will is strengthened by some of the entries in his inventory.

His collection of silver and silver-gilt, while modest by the standards of the richest yeomen of his day, far exceeded in value the pewter more commonly possessed by his contemporaries. Items normally found only in the homes of the gentry catch the eye: his library of thirty-six books, his two desks (one new), a pair of virginals, a wicker chair, £10 worth of silk and drinking glasses all indicate prosperity. His house had eleven rooms, excluding the little closet, vance roof and the two barns which lay in the yard beyond. His great parlour with enough seating for nearly twenty people conjures up visions of Philip entertaining his many relatives and friends, some of whom, like John Balleston (*'very rich in stocke and offereth to buy the farme he useth at 2,050 pounds'*), were used, perhaps, to greater comforts. Sometimes his visitors would have been parish or hundred officials come to receive instructions from their 'cheefe constable', as Philip is described in a Jacobean benevolence list of 1621. One can imagine him setting forth in his best jersey stockings, ruff and silk garters for a meeting of the petty sessions (where two or three of the local JPs met to deal with the problems of crime and local government in their area of Norfolk), or to travel very occasionally to the quarter sessions, there to rub shoulders with the gentry who more frequently held the post of high constable of their hundred. In 1577, in his younger days, we could have seen Philip shouldering his musket and donning his 'headpeece' to attend the muster of the hundred militia. On this particular occasion he was accompanied by Richard Cullyer junior and Edmund Cullyer, all three of them obeying the law of the land which demanded that every able-bodied man between the ages of 16 and 60 should present himself if called upon to do so.

If this picture is too fanciful, too much of a speculation on limited original sources, then the truth may be more sober. His collection of books is worthy of comment. In one sense he had a very typical range of books : the Bible, theological works, John Foxe's *Book of Martyrs* (1571) and the statutes of the realm collected together by William Rastell. His unnamed volumes might well have included some historical works, such as Raleigh's *History of the World* and Michael Dalton's *Country Justice*, a practical manual concerning the duties of county and parish officials which would have eased the difficulty of his tasks as chief constable. But his small library tells us more.

First, he was in a minority among his class in owning such a large number of books; many yeomen possessed none and a majority were illiterate. Secondly, the religious works in his collection indicate the breadth of interest shown by Cullyer in the Protestantism of his day. William Perkins was a most influential member of a group of more extreme Puritans who caused Elizabeth I's government much worry. With Thomas Cartwright as their mentor, and the tireless but elusive John Field keeping them in touch with each other, these men pushed forward their Presbyterian propaganda. Perkins, who died in 1602, was at Christ's College, Cambridge. A zealous converted sinner, he went beyond Calvin's doctrine of predestination to the belief that the Elect could be known to man in this world. A great preacher and author of some 40 works, some of importance, he influenced many men to begin their wills with an exposition of justification by faith and the certainty of their salvation. Some of his views were particularly extreme: he believed that atheists should be put to death. A likeable fellow.

By contrast Richard Greenham represented Puritanism of a more moderate kind. Rector of Dry Drayton, a few miles out on the Huntingdon Road from Cambridge, he made his parish a place of pilgrimage for many afflicted souls. He was at his best as a confessor. Charitable to a fault, he often left himself short of money for his own housekeeping. He was a famed preacher, exhausting himself with the effort. As A.L.Rowse writes (*The England of Elizabeth*, p. 480), *'His gospel was, as so rarely, that of love; his life the achieved life of the Christian saint'*. Beyond his parish he wielded a wide spiritual influence through his sermons and commentaries which were published and continued to be read long after his death.

Why Philip Cullyer possessed the works of these two very different men and what influence they had upon the character of his religious views we cannot know.

How large a household Philip Cullyer maintained is not clear. We know that he married twice, on both occasions in Norwich: first to Maria Slater in 1578 and then in 1580 to Frances Mason, who already had a son John by a previous marriage. His will refers to Frances and to Faith Poynts, a widow, his servant, to whom he left £5, or about four times the annual wage of a best quality female servant in 1625. No doubt Frances' experience in running a household would have ensured that Faith was fully occupied attending to brewing and baking and other household chores, while she could ride alongside her husband to visit outlying properties or friends. All the necessary riding equipment ('furniture') is mentioned as lying in the hall chamber. Philip left his wife comfortably provided for. She was to receive £16 per annum for life, as well as various bedclothes and the pair of virginals!

Philip's house had eleven rooms proper, as well as two barns and, possibly, a stable. In the sixteenth century the hall was usually the main living room in a yeoman's house. Interestingly, the hall is not listed in Cullyer's inventory, and its existence can only be deduced by reference to the *'chamber over the hall'*. No

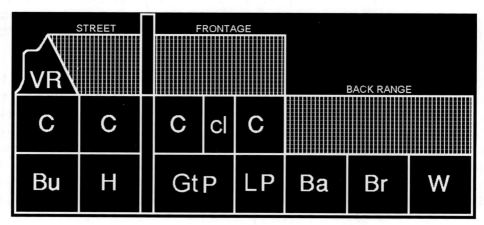

24. Cross-section of Philip Cullyer's house based on his probate inventory. The back range of three outhouses probably ran at 90° to the street frontage.

Ba = BACKHOUSE Br = BREWHOUSE Bu = BUTTERY C = CHAMBER cl = CLOSET
Gt P = GREAT PARLOUR H = HALL LP = LITTLE PARLOUR VR = VANCE ROOF W = WORKSHOP

mention is made of the contents of the hall; it seems to have been replaced by the great parlour as the chief living room of the Cullyer household. Yet the hall existed and possibly shared a common chimney stack with the great parlour. It may be that, as in some other Norfolk farmhouses, the hall was about to become the kitchen, but that the change of use had not occurred because of the limited needs of the old man's household, or because of his conservatism. Alternatively the hall may have been occupied by a relative or lodger, in which case it would have contained none of Philip's own possessions.

What does seem reasonably clear is that it was in the great parlour that the family dined at its framed table and before the open fire, with its collection of fire-place furnishings, that guests were entertained on winter evenings. On this fire the food was probably cooked, for there is reference to an iron jack for turning the spit, although the spits appear to have been kept in the buttery. The buttery may well have acted as a kitchen for the preparation of food before it was cooked. No separate kitchen is mentioned. The great parlour also contained the virginals, a keep or cupboard for the small library of books, a desk – really a portable writing desk cum bible-box – *'where the Greate Bible doe lie'* as well as a futher cupboard and a livery (side) table. No doubt the *'greate cubbord with a greene cover clothe'* was used to display the small collection of silver mentioned at the beginning of the inventory. The pewterware had been consigned to the buttery! His collection of silver and pewter places Cullyer firmly among the more prosperous of his class.

There seems to have been little attempt at decoration or ornamentation in any part of the house. In keeping with his class, the only exceptions are the *'carpett of nedle work'* in the great parlour and the tapestry covering on the bed in the little parlour. No mention is made of wainscotting or window glass which wealthy yeomen sometimes listed in their inventories.

The next most important room after the hall in a yeoman's house was usually the parlour. This contained the best bed and was used as a semi-living-room where more intimate conversation and entertainment could take place. In Cullyer's house the little parlour seems to have occupied this position. Here were no less than three back chairs, as well as five buffet stools. Thus a group of people could gather to converse, three of them sitting on chairs, a form of seating which had not long become common among yeomen. In the not so distant past chairs had been reserved to the master of the house, with all the implied authority traditionally associated with this form of seating. The presence of so many attractively coloured cushions suggests an attempt to make the room both comfortable and pleasing to the eye. The seven glasses, wantonly under-valued by the appraisers, conjure up visions of refreshments accompanying private discussion. Indeed the glasses were still luxury items and very few native glassmakers were in production by 1625, most glasses being made by foreign craftsmen in England. Many glasses were still imported. These glasses were worth at least 20s., perhaps 50% more.

Here, too, one finds a *'faier posted bedstead'* with its furniture, including a feather bed, a comfort which had become quite usual among yeomen by about 1600. William Harrison, writing in his *Description of England* (1587), commented on the improved standard of living of yeomen under Elizabeth I and referred to their bedding as follows:

> *If it were so that our fathers or the good man of the house, had within seven years after his marriage purchased a matteres or flockbed, and thereto a sack of chaffe to rest his head, he thought himself well lodged',* but now, *'every farmer has three or four feather beds so many coverlids and carpets or tapestrie.*

The remaining furniture of the little parlour confirms the impression that this room was important and thus made reasonably comfortable.

Upstairs the chambers or bedrooms include the *'greate parlor chamber'* which was used by Cullyer during his final illness. He refers to *'the great seeled bedstead in the chamber wherein I now lye with the seeled bench belonginge to it'* in his will; in the course of leaving these items to his much favoured godson, Philip Cullyer, the old man could not resist instructing his executor to ensure that they *'shall remaine with my howse for ever'*. Beds had a sentimental as well as a material value in those days. Such items were often passed from one generation to the next.

The great parlour chamber contained a fireplace and the dead man's clothing, but more interesting are the five chests. These chests were most important. In them would be stored everything that must be kept free from dust, or out of reach of hungry mice or prying servants' eyes. The linen would be kept in them, but most important of all would be the ready money and the 'evidences' of Cullyer's right to his property. These documents, in the form of deeds, leases, bonds and other indentures would be Cullyer's protection against scheming landlords and ambitious neighbours, who, with the help of their crafty, sharp-witted lawyers, might try to bring the title of his property into question. One is left in no doubt about the material ambitions of Cullyer himself; his will indicates that he had been accumulating property in the form of land and houses. He had bought three acres of copyhold land in Wymondham from his godson, Robert Cullyer, *'all those meadowes lands and grownds with there appurtenances . . . purchased of John Sewall and Henry Hartstonge gent.', 'all those my howses newelye builte with the yards and grownds... lyinge in Towne Greene Streete'* which he had bought freehold from Stephen Wyseman as recently as 1622 (post-fire rebuilding?) and finally he left his nephew, Philip Cullyer, all the remaining houses and land *'which I bought and purchased of severall persons'*. One is left with the impression that Philip had inherited a hard-headed business approach from his father, grandfather and great-grand-father, resulting in considerable land tenures as well as debts from 'low profile' yeomen such as Valentine Kett. The Cullyers are mentioned several

*25. The Yeoman's House in Town Green, probably a post-fire rebuild, which
Philip Cullyer bought from Stephen Wiseman in 1622 but never occupied.*

times in the Kett family history in the Colman/Rye collection (Norfolk Record Office). In these transactions we see the yeoman playing his part in society as a small, aggressive capitalist, determined to take advantage of every opportunity for increasing his profits and advancing himself socially. One of these chests in the great parlour may have been iron-bound and equipped with several locks to protect the documents which formed the legal basis of Cullyer's property transactions.

Linked with the great parlour chamber was a little closet containing a new desk at which the master of the house may have been attending to his accounts and correspondence before he became too weak to continue. The other chambers were sparsely furnished, as was usual in a yeoman's house. The trendle bed in the little parlour chamber may have been where Cullyer's wife slept while her husband lay dying, or perhaps Faith Poynts, his servant, was transferred to this room to attend her sickly employer.

In the hall chamber, there was a posted bedstead and the kind of articles connected with a farming life one tends to find scattered about a yeoman's house. The buttery chamber and the vance roof, or loft, above it were given over entirely to storing wheat and implements. 'Mixtlinge' was a mixture of rye and wheat which produced a flour variously known as messeldine, messleden or maslin that was very popular with everyone, for even the prosperous gentry did not use the best white flour for everyday purposes. In 1642 Henry Best, a member of the minor gentry in Yorkshire, wrote in his *Farming Book* of the use of maslin, *'The folkes* [workmen's] *pye crusts are made of massledine as our bread is'*. Wheat flour was used for cakes and pastry when there were guests, or when the season called for special feasting. Not only might wheat be sold for a good price, but a heavier bread was considered both more nourishing and more satisfying.

The other rooms mentioned in the inventory were probably joined to the rest of the house at the back (hence 'backhowse') to form an L-shape and ran out alongside the yard. The backs of houses in Wymondham give one a good idea even today of the kind of arrangement of such outhouses. Where there are timber-framed buildings the line of backhouses can be seen; a walk down Brewery Lane, an examination of the backs of houses in Market Street either from the car park behind the old fire station or from Back Lane (appropriately named even in Cullyer's time) will help to form a clearer idea of seventeenth century yards. No. 1 Market Place has a string of backhouses stretching right down to Back Lane. The centre of Wymondham contains many arched entrances, or 'entries', into back yards of this type. These backhouses were furnished to meet the needs their names suggest. Thus Cullyer's brewhouse contains a copper and the 'workhowse' a collection of tools. In the yard and beyond it there were a few more assorted possessions, including wheat, barley and rye in two barns and the horses. Possibly Cullyer had a small quantity of land adjoining his yard which was farmed, but one is tempted to suggest that he obtained his main supplies of food from his other lands. There is no specific mention of 'horse gear' or 'plow gear' which normally appears in inventories of yeomen; nor is any livestock listed. His fellow yeoman, William Algare, left a cart, a plough, a pair of harrows, horse harness, 11 cows, 5 calves, 46 sheep and 22 lambs as well as 4 swine when he died in 1618. And the same is true of other contemporary yeomen such as Loy Agas, William Kent, Robert Fedymonde and Robert Pitcher.

Houses were lighted by candles and the open fire. Most of the candlesticks were of brass or pewter. Cullyer possessed two of each kind. Many yeomen also owned a pair of 'latten' candlesticks made of an alloy closely resembling brass, but containing different proportions of zinc and copper. For example, Robert Pitcher, who died in 1631, left 3 *'lattin'* candlesticks. Sometimes they boasted two silver ones.

In general, one is left with the impression that Philip was a yeoman whose wealth was in the making; that he preferred to live relatively simply and to invest his money in land, houses and presumably livestock rather than in more elaborate furnishings for his own house.

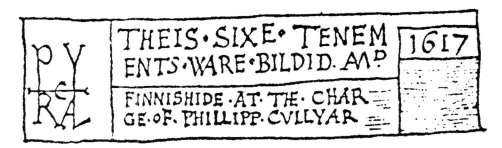

26. Rebus & inscription attached to the almshouses built by Philip Cullyer in the yard opposite the Yeoman's House in Town Green. Drawn by Thomas Martin in 1722.

While Cullyer did much to advance his worldly wealth by legitimate means, he was not slow to assist the town and its inhabitants when the need arose. His record speaks for itself. He lent money to the town on several occasions: £25 7s to rebuild the market cross and £30 towards the rebuilding of the schoolhouse. He built a set of six almshouses (in what is now known as Cullyer's Yard) at his own expense which he gave to the town to replace others *'decayed in the fire'*. At the advanced age of sixty-four he travelled several times to London as the payment of his expenses reveals: *'Delivered to Phillip Cullyer att his goeinge to London aboute the fynes for the Prince his Highnes mannor £1 12s 0d.'* In this he was successful and manorial tenants in the King's Manor suffered no increase for the renewal of tenancies. Finally, as John Forbie, rector of Attleborough, recorded in 1625 in an epitaph to Cullyer:

> *He was verie charitablie mynded and cloathed every yeere at Christmas longe before his death twentie poore children with all things from the head to the foote. [...] He did also feast them whom he did then cloath att the same Christmas. And brought them that daye to the church and gave God all the thanks.*

The relief of poverty

Tudor governments had gradually learned to distinguish between the wandering bands of 'sturdy vagabonds' who would not work, able-bodied beggars capable of work who could not find any and the *'aged, poor and impotent persons'* who could not support themselves. The first group needed to be forcibly *'set on work'*. The able-bodied were to be provided with the basic tools and raw materials (wool, hemp, flax and iron are mentioned in the Act of 1576) with which to work in their homes. The impotent poor ideally required support without condition.

Initial reliance on the charitable giving of alms by parishioners to support the deserving poor gave way by 1572 to the levying of a compulsory parish poor rate from which relief was organised by the churchwardens and newly created overseers of the poor. The whole system reached its maturity in the Elizabethan Poor Relief Act of 1601 which was to last in essentials until 1834.

In Wymondham the Town Book contains the chief surviving record of poor relief in operation between the Armada and the eighteenth century. [All quotations in the remainder of this section and its successor come from the Town Book.] The Town Lands Charity was set up in 1559 by Elizabeth I who granted control of the revenue of properties and lands formerly belonging to the Abbey and the religious guilds to a group of feoffees (trustees of land). This grant was confirmed by the court of the Queen's Manor in 1561. Apart from maintaining a free grammar school, the feoffees were expected, according to Blomefield, to devote their remaining funds to other charitable purposes, one of which became poor relief.

Part of the charity's money supplemented the poor rates and the 'collector', who was appointed annually, saw to its distribution, apart from a brief spell around 1660 when lump sums were handed directly to the four overseers. This additional source of funds was very much needed as the evidence quoted earlier on page 58 for the level of poverty in the town in 1622 shows.

68

Until the late 1640s the feoffees provided only two forms of relief for all poor people: corn, or bread and firewood, at a subsidised price. In 1598–99 William Cullyer was paid 15s 4d *'for bakyng of breade for the pore folke'* and in 1605–06 the town bought wood to sell to the poor at the reduced prioce of 2d a faggot (bundle).

Otherwise, relief from charity funds tended to be directed to the particular needs of a small number of individual paupers. One major preoccupation concerned supporting orphans and illegitimate or 'town' children. Some were fostered by local women like Joan Lenard who was paid 6s 8d *'for kepyng one of John Frances chyldren'* and the town also paid for poor children to enter apprenticeships. Thus in 1608–9, the vestry paid £1 5d for *'the appareling of the wydowe Thowelldelles sonne to putt him to syvice as an apprentice'*. The Town Book often gives a detailed account of the clothing provided, as when Gibbes went to work for Thomas Kett in 1610–11. His hose (probably still breeches rather than stockings at this date) and linings cost 4s 4d, shirts 2s 6d, doublet and its linings 2s 10d, jerkin cloth and buttons for it 4s 3d, and a pair of netherstocks (stockings from the thigh downwards) and a pair of shoes 2s 10d. Anthony Pile was paid 4s for making the doublet, jerkin, hose and shirts. The total came to £1 9d, almost equal to the annual wages of a female servant who lived in all found.

Sometimes it is clear that the town wished to rid itself of responsibility for an illegitimate child or perhaps a child born to someone visiting the town who threatened to stay and become a charge on the rates.

1617–18: *Item paid to John Shoo the remaynder behinde for takinge of a towne childe so he is paid all for the same*	£2	0s	0d

The town paid for many types of medical attention. Some entries in the accounts are brief but underline the pitiful state into which the poor could fall: *'in a consumption'*, *'with the falinge sicknes'*, *'almost starved'*, *'healing of . . . toes that rotted of'* and *'Gallardes wife in childbed without any succor'*. The feoffees could show considerable compassion and dig deep into their funds. This could include paying for treatment of the sick at one of the five lazar houses outside the gates of Norwich, as in 1617–18 when William Mappes's daughter was admitted to the house at the Magdalen Gate *'having the fallinge sickenes'* (epilepsy) at a cost of £3 10s. All manner of accidents and misfortunes were paid for:

1598–99: *Item payd to Brownes wyfe for helyng the chylderens heades beyng skalde* [scabby scalp disease, possibly ringworm]		5s	0d
1602–3: *Sicknes. Geven to diverse pore people in the tyme that ther howses were visited with the infection* [plague]	£3	6s	6d
1605–6: *Delyvered & geven to a pore prentise, the sonne of Christian Smythe, & servante to Christopher Browne, being lame & diseased, towardes his going to the bathe*	£1	0s	0d

1617–18: *Item payd to Mr Wylliam Wells for the cuttinge of*
Lemondes legg which the surgeons had £3 6s 8d

And more vividly:

1646–47: *Given Henry Smithes wife to releive her legg beinge*
broake with 2 dogges commynge out of Markett 6d

The funeral expenses of paupers were paid (2–3s), principally for a sheet to 'wind' the body in, and others were helped by the town to recover basic and essential possessions. In 1630–31 William Littleproud was paid a shilling to redeem his bed from Jacobb and a year later Thomas Agas was given 1s 2d to restore the long saw to John Flowerdewe that John had pawned.

After the Civil Wars of the 1640s, the character of relief changed. More paupers were paid more regularly. These were usually smaller sums (a few pence each time) and Town Book entries give little or no explanation for them. Distributions of clothing, or money in place of clothing, become a feature of relief, e.g.

The names of the poore cloathed in the yeare 1657

Mens coats	Thomas Bell	Westcoats	Margarett Woodfall
	Elias Holgrave		Elizabeth Taylor
	Robert Higgs		Kath Neavell
	old Hayles		Rose English
			Widdow Woodcock
			Widdow Thurston
Britches	Robert Cobb		Joane Swayne
	Robert Jackson		Neaves wife
		Little coats	Townesends boy
			Locks boy
			Jane Rust a petticoat

At the same time £1 4s 6d was shared between fourteen 'poore people that had no cloathes'.

Controlling the poor

Fear of 'sturdy beggars' had first motivated the Tudors to seek to control those poor who would not obey the poor law. To this end JPs had been instructed from 1576 to set up houses of correction, or bridewells, in their local areas. Wymondham's bridewell was set up at the latest in 1619 to punish those who would not work freely in return for relief. In 1631, ordered by local JPs, the headboroughs set up a workhouse by clearing Richard Male and John Inglishe from their town houses in Town Green. This provided a place where the homeless poor could be 'set on work'. Richard Smythe was made keeper of the new workhouse and lent £40 against the security of his own house *'for a stocke to sett poore people over worke'*. In addition the town bought some basic equipment for spinning, including a 'twistering' mill, a form of plying machine, *(see Fig. 30)* which needed rebuilding.

1630–31: *For twoe payer of wolle combes delivered to Smythe*	9s	0d
For a payer of trussells & a hurdell to beat wolle on	1s	6d
For a twisteringe myll & necessaries to it videlicet 4 sett of bobbyns & 48ty cokes an iron cranke to score yarne 43 spiers 2 trundells & 8 swiftes delivered him £3	0s	6d
Paide for takinge downe the myll & settinge it up & for a new dore & other worke done by Thomas Agas	6s	0d
Paide Halloway for a newe locke & mendinge a locke & stelinge & mendinge 44 spiers for the twistringe myll	3s	2d
For halfe a pounde of wyer for that myll		6d
For brasse to frame into the myll & to Fearme & Inglish for helpinge	1s	0d

Accompanying these changes Wymondham took steps to prevent incomers becoming a burden on the poor rates. In 1635 220 people attended the court leet of Grishaugh to witness the passing of a byelaw to prevent unwanted settlement in the town. In 1662 the Settlement Act was passed. The most important poor law between 1601 and 1834, it laid down that any stranger settling in a parish could be removed unless he could rent a tenement of £10, or prove that he would cost the parish nothing. Thus the force of law was given to the existing practice of Wymondham parish constables: in one recorded case an unwanted person was dumped over the boundary into Hethersett. The new law led to great cruelty as many defenceless people who had fallen on hard times were passed from one parish to another en route to one where they had a right of settlement. For a short time in 1673–74, the town employed Robert Dey to inform the vestry of people who were *'newly come to inhabitt in the towne'*. In return he was paid 6d per person for his trouble.

Echoes of the Irish Rebellion and the Civil War

In 1641 a major rebellion of the native Catholics occurred in Ireland. The policy of Thomas Wentworth, Earl of Strafford, the king's Lord Deputy in Ireland, had alienated most of the important English ruling groups from the royal government without persuading the natives to accept English Protestant control and the occupation of Ireland by a foreign settler class.

As the scale of the conflict and the atrocities committed by the rebels grew, the stories of outrage reaching England became ever more exaggerated. Soon victims of the rebellion arrived in Wymondham and told the townsmen of their experiences in heart-rending terms. Those claiming relief from the Wymondham vestry were usually described as gentlemen or gentlewomen. Clergy seemed popular recipients and women and children figured prominently. The following Town Book extracts indicate the nature of the successful applications:

1641–42: *Gyven to Daniell Harber generosus his wife & thre*
children being dryven out of Ireland by the rebells whoe lost
£200 per annum and £700 in money & goodes   2s   0d
1647–1648: *Given to M^{ris} Mary Kinge Ellen Kinge & Judith Browne*
3 gentlewomen whose husbondes & 6 children were slayne & all there
goodes taken by Irish rebells. Kinge was Doctor of Divinity   1s   0d

Often the refugees presented 'certificates' or formal letters from important people confirming their need for charitable relief, all the better if they were local men of good standing.

1647–1648: *Given M^{ris} Mary Seamore & 11 children stript*
by the rebells in Irelond of £1000 & upward her husbond
*slain & 2 servants slayne. She was sent by Mr Weld**   1s   0d
[*Thomas Weld, a wealthy lawyer and trusted servant of the town]

In other cases, support came from national bodies such as the Westminster Assembly of Divines, a strongly Presbyterian body, mainly of clergy, formed in 1643 *'to be consulted with by the Parliament, for the settling of the government of the Church'.*

1645–1646: *To Beniamyn Hyrne an aged minister who lost £500*
in Irelond beside his spirituall lyvinge worth £70 per annum
certefied under the handes of sondry of the Assembly of Divines   1s   0d

By the later stages of the Civil War, pence rather than shillings were being handed out. It seems that initial generosity gave way to more circumspect giving!

In 1642 the Civil War broke out between King Charles I and Parliament. East Anglia was a source of strength to the Parliamentary side and yet Norfolk experienced only one short spell of fighting, the siege of King's Lynn which declared for the royalists in August 1643 and surrendered to the Earl of Manchester in September *'to avoid the effusion of blood'*. While Wymondham's sympathies tended to be with the Roundheads, there was a less happy side to these intolerant times. A contingent of 500 soldiers from Essex on their way to join Manchester *'as they came through Windham pulled down the organs in the church'*.

Wymondham was not close to any major battles and thus what we can hear through local sources are mainly distant echoes of the Civil War. The second volume of the Town Book (1627–1662) gives an impression of how the Civil War affected Wymondham people. While parishes were required to relieve maimed soldiers and to equip those setting out to fight in wars, the incidence of claims upon local charity was higher with a domestic rather than a foreign war in progress. In 1642–43 three soldiers *'that went away with Captayne Harvy'* were paid a total of £3 10s and widow Agas had to pay a parliamentary subsidy and towards *'setting forth of horse for the state'*. Not everyone went willingly to war. In 1645–46 Arthyr Plowman, Jacob, Edward Parke, John Moore and Raph Jesipp were paid the sum of £4 8s 6d *'which they being constables had laid out for pressinge & apparilinge of souldiors'*.

Relief was given to *'a poore lame souldior'* who had been fighting unsuccessfully to defend Newark against the royalist Prince Rupert. The town paid for winding sheets and the burial of less fortunate soldiers. Thomas King, the parish clerk and sexton, received 6d for *'ringinge & grave makinge'* for a dead soldier. A parliamentary land tax had to be paid by the vestry on land it rented out.

Entries in the Town Book may hint at how the headboroughs viewed the royalist army. In 1644–45 3s was given to *'Mr Raynoldes from whome the Cavalers toke £2000 & £300 per annum'* and *'Mr William Cave a Wiltshire minister who was plundred & imprisoned by Prince Ruperts army'* received 3s a year later. At the same time Thomas Auger is described as newly released *'out of prison from the enemyes garrison at Oxford'*.

When a parliamentary general passed through Wymondham the town's traditional hospitality and respect for important visitors were shown.

1645–1646: *Paid for sack* [Spanish white wine] *for my Lord Generall* [Thomas Fairfax?] *& his company when they cam through towne*   6s   0d
Given Kinge for ringinge that day   2s   6d

Pirates

If civil war was not trouble enough, the Town Book lists payments made to those who had suffered at the hands of pirates. 'Dunkirks', or 'Dunkirkers', were pirates marauding in the Channel.

1641–42: *Gyven to Mr Johnson a Scotshe man his wife & one childe beinge robbed by the Dunkirkes of one hundred & fiftie powndes*   1s   0d

In the Mediterranean, the Barbary pirates, whose main base was the port of Algiers, rapidly increased in number in the first half of the seventeenth century. They were notorious for kidnapping, ransoming and enslaving mariners. Thus it was unsurprising that in England pirates in the Mediterranean were often referred to as 'Turks'.

1645–46: *To George Kidemore who was 7 yere 6 monthes prisoner with the Turkes who lost in the shipp called The Neptune of Deale in Kent £1800 & £500 beinge part owner of it*   1s   0d

Economic life

Wymondham society in the seventeenth century was different from ours in one major respect. While many occupations were becoming specialised, farming activities were not restricted to those who called themselves yeoman or husbandman. Many inhabitants grew some of their food while earning money in other ways. They rented land from which they might sell surplus produce and also earned money from a main occupation as, for example, a blacksmith, cobbler, mason or weaver. Thus the inventory of Thomas Moore, a butcher, reveals in 1629 that he had an essential piece of farming equipment, a plough and the wheels to go with it. Likewise Thomas Cole, linen weaver, in his inventory of 1618 had a plough with its *'furniture'*. Prosperous inhabitants such as merchants, yeomen and gentlemen tended to own land which they might farm or rent out. Husbandmen would generally be tenants of land while tradesmen might rent or have none. The poor who owned or rented no land were dependent on lowly paid, often seasonal, work, their relatives, or charity for survival.

Agriculture was the foundation of the local economy. The parish lay in the boulder clay region of East Anglia and the soils varied from heavy clay on the plateau to lighter, sandier ones of the valleys of the River Tiffey and its tributaries which cut through it. By 1600 Wymondham still had as many as nine open fields which possessed areas of strip cultivation on the lighter soils alongside the increasing number of enclosures, many put down to grass to provide feed for cattle. There were probably as many as 5,000 acres of open field, 3,000 acres of common and hundreds of acres of both meadow and woodland.

In 1596 the farming activities in the area were described in State Papers collected by W.Rye as ' . . . *sustayned cheefelye by grasseways, by Dayries and rearinge cattell . . .* ' in an area ' . . . *able to maintayne itself with Corne and to afforde an overplus to their neyboures of Suffolk'*. About half of the parish was devoted to meadows and pasture and the other half to arable farming. Perhaps the earliest complete tithe book for Wymondham dating from 1647 reveals that by acreage of great tithes 34% was devoted to mixed crops, 22% to barley, 15% to wheat and 2% to summer ley (temporary grassland). Among the small tithes, cattle fattening, dairying and the production of wool were also important. The virtue of income from dairy products was that it helped tide farmers over poor harvest years. The number of animals tithed were 756 calves, 1,045 lambs, 1,308 (estimated) ewes, 2,645 (estimated) sheep. 968½ acres of grass and £27 worth of herbage were also listed. In addition there was plentiful common land for grazing sheep and still fairly abundant supplies of timber as the rebuilding of houses after the fire of 1615 showed. Apart from seven woods mentioned in documents, there was timber growing on meadow land, an example being Teddes Close which produced much of the timber and firewood belonging to the town itself.

In addition to tithe books other major sources of information about local farming are wills, leases and inventories. Wills can provide clues about farming methods through bequests of land and animals, often accompanied by rules about how particular resources such as woodland are to be used. John Balleston, gentleman, instructed in his will of 1661 that Emm, his widow, could take coppice-wood to use as firewood or to sell if she needed the income. Appropriate timber could be taken for house repairs. Sometimes 'hedgebot' was mentioned, the right to take wood from the commons to repair fences. Exception clauses in leases might stipulate that certain trees, for example *'100 best stands'* (young trees left standing) were to be left for the landlord to fell when they were sufficiently mature. Landlords could impose conditions of other kinds such as the requirement to make *'a good & sufficient ditche'* of given dimensions set with a double hedge of hawthorn round a tenant's field. They could also lease out rights only indirectly associated with agriculture. In 1586 for 40s per annum Jeffery Drake, a tailor, took up a 21 year lease of a third of the profits arising from the markets and fairs of Wymondham together with the profits of all strays of *'horse, neate, sheepe or other cattell'* within Wymondham. These rights belonged to the lordship of the

27. *'Cottage at Wymondham', an impression of rural living conditions by Robert Dixon in 1811 which could apply to post-medieval times generally.*

Manor of Cromwells.

Inventories often contain detailed information about crops in store or standing in the field, animals, implements and basic machinery such as carts, ploughs and harrows. They can tell us what is happening at different seasons of the year depending on when they were made. What seems to emerge is a picture of mixed farming in which the most profitable activities were keeping sheep and dairying. However, only large landowners like Sir Anthony Drury of Besthorpe and Sir Philip Wodehouse of Kimberley had anything approaching sizeable flocks of sheep. Wodehouse's inventory in December 1623 listed 420 lambs and only 30 sheep while Drury in November 1638 had wethers, ewes and lambs worth £36. By contrast Framlingham Gawdy in the 1650s was running three flocks at Mid Harling, Thorpe and North Harling totalling nearly 1,600 animals. This puts into perspective the largest number found in early seventeenth-century inventories: 46 sheep and 22 lambs belonging to William Algare when he died in April 1618, 28 sheep of Robert Pitcher (1631) and 21 sheep of Thomas Scarles (1671). It seems possible that the sheep of less prosperous farmers were run with the large flocks of the gentry. Animals and grazing rights for a given number or stint often came with rented land. The lease book of Sir Edward Clere (1577–99), admittedly of the later sixteenth century, reveals that Robert Lawnde rented 52½ acres 'with the stocke . . . namelie twelve good mylche beastes and one hundred sheep called wethers together with the libertie of sheepepasture & sheepe keeping in and upon the common viz. 100 ewe ware or sheepe with theire followers' (about 180 animals).

Dairying and the animals required are frequently mentioned in documents. Thus Loy Agas's inventory dated 1611 shows that he had 7 milk cows, 2 of which were with calves and 3 were pregnant. William Algare left 11 cows, 2 weanings and 3 yearling calves while Thomas Scarles owned 9 cows, 2 bullocks, a bull and 2 calves. These men were not only producing large quantities of milk but also cheese. For example, Thomas Scarles had cheese worth £10 in his dairy chamber which probably represented at least 200 individual cheeses given that a small cheese then cost 6d. To process the milk he produced, Loy Agas had a dairy which contained a cheese press, 4 vats which acted as moulds in which the cheese was pressed, 2 breads or covers for the vats, 12 milk bowls, a milk keeler or cooler, a milk tub, a churn with its staff and a cheese keeler.

Other animals necessary to arable farming were horses or draught steers (oxen) to pull carts and ploughs. Horses cost about £3 each and oxen half as much while cows averaged out at £2 10s. Two horses were required to pull a two-wheeled seventeenth-century plough and could do so with greater speed and reliability than oxen but were relatively costly to maintain. Other animals that were popular included pigs, chickens and turkeys. Chickens, which were cheap and therefore in popular demand, were often kept in large numbers. Feeding horses and cows through the winter required adequate supplies of hay supplemented at times with oats and barley. Inventories mention hay stacks: Thomas Scarles had three valued at £6 each. Farmers were looking for new sources of animal feed. One of the earliest known references to the field-growing of turnips occurs in a tithe book of 1653. Robert Skepper had 15 acres of turnips in Burtoftes with which to feed his bullocks but this was an experiment and it was not until the later years of the seventeenth century that turnips began to be grown more generally. Animal dung was a principal source of fertiliser and was often applied by folding sheep on arable after harvest to tread in their droppings.

A selection of occupations of Wymondham people from seventeenth century documents gives some idea of the developing commercial life of the town:

baker	draper	haberdasher	mason	turner
beer brewer	felt maker	husbandman	mercer	wool chapman
blacksmith	gardener	labourer	miller	wool draper
butcher	glazier	linen weaver	spooner	yeoman
clerk	glover	locksmith	tailor	
cordwainer	grocer	mariner	thatcher	

Apart from agriculture three industries in particular were characteristic of Wymondham: wood-turning and making everyday items in wood, textiles and beer-brewing. The fairly generous supply of wood available in the south of the parish encouraged the development of crafts such as wood-turning and spoon making, the latter giving rise to the hamlet of Spooner Row. Carvings of spoons, taps and spindles decorate the external woodwork of the new market cross of 1617–18 and the town's arms show a crossed spoon and spigot. However, while the products of this industry have long since perished, there are documentary references to spooners and some of them achieved a modest prosperity. Henry Colman the elder who died in 1624 left a mansion house, four acres of meadow, several closes and £25 in bequests. In 1637 two Wymondham spooners, Nicholas Howlett and Richard Blome, travelled to Holland in search of work. Robert Blome, perhaps a relative of Richard, in his will of 1644 left land and tenements to his wife for the education and upkeep of their three children.

Wymondham appears to have benefited from the revival of the Norwich textile industry following the influx of Dutch and Walloon weavers after 1565. They brought new textiles and the expansion of business was described by the mayor of Norwich in 1575 as setting on work 'our owne people within the cittie, as also a grete number of people here 20 miles about the cittie'. Wymondham did outwork for Norwich, especially by combing and spinning worsted yarn for large manufacturers in the city, while there are references to worsted weavers, linenweavers, combers and spinsters in contemporary documents. And yet while spinning wheels and clock reels are mentioned fairly frequently in inventories and are often employed to supplement incomes earned in very different main occupat-

28. Carved spoons and spigots on the Market Cross, illustrating the woodworking tradition in Wymondham which probably gave Spooner Row its name.

ions, looms are fairly infrequently encountered. Most references to weavers in the later seventeenth century are to linen weavers such as Christopher Curtis, who in 1676 had three pair of looms, a winding wheel, linen valued at £8 5s and a large quantity of hemp worth £30 5s. The total value of his inventory was £119 4s 10d.

The material used by linen weavers was not flax but hemp and there are references to hemp being grown in Wymondham and hemp seed being tithed.

In an age before tea and coffee had become national drinks and while water supplies were often untrustworthy, the common drink for most people was a weak form of ale or beer. Much of this was made in brew houses attached to the rear range of houses as part of the cycle of household activities. However, alehouses had existed from medieval times and had been licensed by Justices of the Peace since 1552 to prevent abuses and public disorder. Some of the places serving ale were inns such as the King's Head, the Griffin and the Hart on Market Street which served the steady flow of travellers along the route between London and Norwich. The Grishaugh leet appointed ale tasters to check the quality of local brews and in 1600 three of the town's brewers were prosecuted at the quarter sessions for brewing *'contrary to statute'*. So numerous were the alehouses in Wymondham that in 1622 there were complaints that the town's 33 establishments were sucking *'the thrifte from a nomber of those poore people'* and adding seriously to the problem of poverty.

Emigration from Wymondham in the early seventeenth century

Records exist which show significant emigration from Norfolk in the early seventeenth century to both Holland and New England. While the reasons for the emigration to both areas were similar – to escape the prevailing religious regime in Norfolk and to become more prosperous – there was a huge difference between the journeys and the ultimate destination.

The journey from Great Yarmouth to Holland usually took less than 24 hours. Holland in the early seventeenth century had a booming economy and welcomed skilled immigrants. While strong trade links had existed between Norfolk and the Low Countries for centuries, these had been greatly strengthened by the substantial immigration from the Low Countries in the late sixteenth century which resulted from the war of revolt against Spanish rule and religious persecution. In the late sixteenth century, it is estimated in Norwich that out of a total population of 16,000 some 6,000 were Dutch and Walloons.

Records exist for the years 1637 to 1639 showing some 600 people crossed in those years from Great Yarmouth to Holland, of whom 34 came from Wymondham. Travellers were required to give a reason for their journey and these show both the close family ties that existed and that prospective emigrants could decide to return to Norfolk if they wished.

Travellers from Wymondham included:
Rebeca Hamon, a widow aged 42, who intended *'to go into Holland to visit a sister of hers living there & to retorne in 3 monthes'*.
Anne Coper, aged 49, who intended to *'passe into Holland to her husband whoe*

dwelleth their and to stay there with him'.

Nicholas Howlett, a spoonmaker aged 31, who intended to *'passe into Holland to seeke worke for 3 mounthes'*.

John Watts, a feltmaker aged 31, who intended to *'goe into Holland & upon liking there to live or retorne in 3 monethes'*.

Judith Woodshed, a knitter aged 30, who intended to *'passe into Holland to live there as a Servant or at her owne hand other to retorne a gane'*.

Some of the reasons given were not totally honest as they avoid any mention of religious convictions. After 1635 over a hundred people are said to have fled from the Forehoe hundred alone as a result of the campaign of Matthew Wren, the Bishop of Norwich, against the Puritan element in Norfolk. An English church was set up in Rotterdam, and included in the founding members were James Gedney, and Stephen and Thomas Gooch from Wymondham.

Both a Thomas and a Stephen Gooch are recorded as passing into Holland in February 1638, to visit their *'father and mother & to retorne in moneth or twoe'*.

Emigrating to New England was an entirely different prospect. The journey itself took some eight to twelve weeks and travellers knew it was very unlikely they would ever return to Norfolk.

The first settlement in New England at Plymouth was founded in 1620, and by 1630 there were some 1,500 English settlers. During the 'Great Migration' of the 1630s, a further 14,000 crossed to New England.

There were economic reasons for emigrating, and Captain John Smith had given an alluring description of New England – *'Here every man may be master of his own labour & land . . . and by industry grow rich'*.

However, the main reason would have been the wish to set their own religious practice, and the remoteness of New England meant they were far from the reach of persecuting bishops. Under the leadership of John Winthrop, Massachusetts became a virtual republic where Puritan men could elect their own Governor, supervise one another and enact a code of laws derived from the Bible. American records show that some 14 people emigrated from Wymondham during the period 1633 to 1638 to the new settlement of Hingham, Massachusetts in New England.

These were

> Thomas Hobart, his wife and three children
> Stephen Lincoln, his wife and son Steven
> Samuel Packer, his wife and child
> Thomas Lincoln and Jeremiah Moore
> Richard Baxter (servant of Francis James of Hingham)

All the men (apart from Richard Baxter) received grants of land and appear to have prospered.

Thomas Hobart received several grants of land, had eleven children and died in 1689. Stephen Lincoln died in 1658, leaving an estate valued at £179 to his son Steven as well as livestock and other assets.

In Thomas Lincoln's will made in 1681, his wife Margaret and eight children are named. His sons were carpenters and farmers. His daughter Elizabeth married Daniel Lincoln, whose brother Mordecai is claimed to be an ancestor of President Abraham Lincoln.

Samuel Packer moved to West Bridgwater, Massachusetts, where he was a constable and a tavernkeeper.

Jeremiah Moore moved to Boston, had 3 children and at his death in 1650 his goods were valued at £87 17s 0d.

It is likely that many more emigrated to the New World but their records are not yet identified. In total during the seventeenth century it is estimated some 21,000 English men and women emigrated to New England, 120,000 to the Virginia area and 190,000 to the West Indies. However, by 1700 the total English population was estimated at 91,000 in New England, 85,000 in the Virginia area and 33,000 in the West Indies. This was largely the result of the far healthier climate in New England than in the Caribbean.

CHAPTER FIVE

Nonconformity

The national Religious Census taken in March 1851 showed that in the town of Wymondham with its associated hamlets, a wide variety of worship was available across the denominational spectrum. Indeed, there were a greater number of different religious groups than in any other Norfolk town. The congregations recorded were Independent, Baptist, Quaker, Wesleyan Methodist, Primitive Methodist, Latter Day Saints and non-denominational as well as Church of England.

In the confusion of the English Civil War in the seventeenth century and the imprisonment and execution of the high church Archbishop Laud, many of those who had taken refuge in the Low Countries as religious exiles, felt the occasion had come to return to England. In the mid-1640s, a number of Independent (later known as Congregational) congregations were established in Norfolk and Suffolk, including one set up in 1646 by *'the godly party'* in Wymondham. This congregation felt itself to be hampered by its inexperience and lack of confidence to manage its church affairs. In consequence, it wrote to the Independent church at Yarmouth for direction and advice. The congregation also pointed out that as a result of their small numbers, there was not enough money to maintain a pastor. The letter was carried by a John Money.

Nevertheless, the congregation continued to meet. John Money became their minister and in 1652 the Independent church in Wymondham was officially formed. Money remained its pastor for about four decades as well as being appointed parish minister in the parish reforms of 1652 until his ejection at the Restoration. He was greatly admired for his skill in preaching especially as *'he never put pen to paper for his sermons, but wrought all in his head'*.

The first instance of a Quaker presence in the town was in October 1654. This was a time when Quakers were travelling from their base in the north of England in order to attract new supporters. A Quaker missionary, Richard Hubberthome, attended one of John Money's services and spoke to the congregation after the sermon. He was arrested, taken to Norwich and there imprisoned. Another worker was quickly sent by George Fox and this missionary held a number of religious meetings in Wymondham. So great was his success that when Fox visited Wramplingham the following year, one thousand people gathered to hear him. However, Quakers attracted hostility even during the rule of Cromwell and were in constant danger of imprisonment.

With the king's return in 1660, all groups of Dissenters were liable to persecution and, in consequence, met in secret. It was only with the Declaration of Indulgence in 1672 that Dissenters were officially tolerated on condition they obtained licences for the premises they used for worship. Licences were obtained for Presbyterian, Quaker and four Independent congregations in the town. This leniency was temporary and soon persecution began again. However, in 1689, the Act of Toleration finally allowed Dissenters to meet together for worship and to build themselves permanent premises.

The Quakers anticipated the Act by erecting a meeting house in 1687 just outside the town and close to the mediaeval chapel which had previously served as a meeting place. It was a brave venture. The new building was domestic in outward appearance so as not to attract unwonted attention. It was formally licensed for worship in 1689 and appears to have gathered a large congregation with more than 92 separate donations from individuals for the new building.

The Independents built a chapel at Wattisfield (?Wattlefield) at the end of the century whilst, in 1715, another was built at Fairland in the town by Roger Gay, one of the church deacons. In 1815 this building underwent substantial rebuilding and enlargement in order to accommodate its growing congregation. It is now the United Reformed Church.

During the first four decades of the eighteenth century, there was a general decline in interest in religion throughout the country, but by mid-century, there was again a quickening in religious life. Perhaps this was not before time in Wymondham for the Independent minister, James Davidson, wrote in 1761, *'I purpose to leave this place . . . for the health and support of my numerous family, as also on account of the dreadful profaneness of the Town and Parish'*. Much of the stimulus for the religious revival came from the strenuous work of John Wesley and his followers.

The first evidence of Methodist activity was the visit of the young itinerant preacher [minister] Richard Reece. He noted in his journal in March 1789 that he *'rode from Diss to Spooney Row and preached to a good company there'*. He went on to Suton to preach again the following day.

Like other dissenting groups when they first began meeting for worship, the first Methodists held services in cottages, barns, outbuildings, workshops and other temporary premises. They only began to build when their future seemed assured. A chapel was erected in Spooner Row in 1814, but it was another decade before there was a purpose-built Wesleyan Methodist chapel in the town. It was situated in Friarscroft Lane. It belonged to the Norwich circuit, but, like so many other Norfolk congregations, broke away from the Wesleyan Methodist Connexion in the mid nineteenth century and joined the Wesleyan Reformers, a new group which opposed what they saw as the autocratic authority of the Wesleyan hierarchy. This congregation did not last long and by 1874 a Wesleyan congregation was once again meeting for worship in the town.

Primitive Methodism, another breakaway movement from the main Wesleyan tradition, arrived in Norfolk in 1821. By 1823 a congregation had been assembled in Wymondham and, from 1832, built itself a succession of chapels. There were also Primitive Methodist congregations at Suton and Silfield.

All religious groups benefited from Methodist activity and a Baptist congregation was formed in Wymondham in 1796.

In 1747, Robert Cremer, vicar of Wymondham, conducted a census by calling at every house in the parish to enquire as to the religious affiliation of the inhabitants. He found that from a total of 686 families, 21 were Quakers and 33 were other Dissenters. In contrast, in a reply to a Bishop's questionnaire in 1827, the vicar, the Reverend William Papillon, estimated that of the 5,000 people in the parish, 2,000 attended the Established Church while 1,500 were Dissenters and another 1,500 were unable or unwilling to attend any place of worship. The proportion of nonconformists in Wymondham had greatly increased over the course of eighty years.

By the later part of the nineteenth century and early years of the twentieth, many of the Wymondham congregations were wealthy enough to embark on ambitious building programmes. A large Primitive Methodist chapel on Town Green was opened in 1871 and a small chapel at Suton in 1889, the Wesleyans built a chapel in

29. United Reformed Church (formerly Congregational), the Fairland.

Damgate Street in 1879, the Baptists engaged the services of the Norwich architect, A.F. Scott to erect a church in Queen Street in 1909 to succeed their chapel in Friarscroft Lane, whilst in the 1890s the Congregationalists made substantial alterations to their church and then gave the building a new facade in 1910. The Salvation Army built a small place of worship in the town. It was converted to a shop when the congregation moved first to Pople Street and then to a brick building in Queen Street. The Mormon congregation, on the other hand, experienced losses with several emigrations to Salt Lake City as well as a decline in interest amongst those who remained. The cause was officially disbanded in 1890.

The Nonconformist churches flourished and new chapels were built by the Plymouth Brethren (Browick Road, 1833), the Primive Methodists (Silfield, 1868 and Town Green, 1871), the Wesleyans (Wattlefield *c*.1833 and Damgate Street 1879), the Independents (Congregational) who enlarged the Fairland chapel in 1877 and the Baptists (Queen Street, completed in 1911). *Hunt's Directory* also referred to a clay building in a small field opposite the Bridewell *'used by Christians who belong to no denomination'*.

This chapel was in fact used by the Plymouth Brethren. At one time it was ministered by George Jeckell, who had given up his last post as Anglican curate at the parish church. His son (born in the vicarage before the change in religion) became the well-known architect and designer, Thomas Jeckyll (1827–1881). Thomas (who changed the spelling of the surname), amongst other works, restored Becket's Chapel and designed wrought-iron gates which can be seen at Sandringham.

During the twentieth century, the Plymouth Brethren meeting place, which was the successor to the non-denominational congregation of the 1851 census, was closed and converted to a house. So, too, was the Quaker meeting house although there is now, once again, a Quaker meeting in the town. The Salvation Army premises were converted to an electricity station. In 1932, when the Methodist strands united, the Wesleyan chapel was sold to become a Masonic temple and the congregation joined the Primitive Methodists at Town Green, thus once again presenting a united Methodism in the town.

CHAPTER SIX

The Eighteenth Century

After the tumult of the Reformation and Kett's Rebellion in the sixteenth century and the Civil War in the seventeenth, life in Wymondham in the eighteenth century was quieter, although war and its local results were not altogether absent. Norwich was only nine miles away and at the beginning of the eighteenth century was the second city in the country with a thriving textile industry and a booming economy. However, later in the century there were bread riots in Norwich and after the French Revolution it became known as the 'Jacobin City' due to its support for revolutionary ideas. These events and ideas must have been discussed in Wymondham which was linked to the city though its own textile workers, through the daily traffic going to and from London and other towns on the main road, and through the necessary links with markets and shops.

As we have seen, the first unofficial census was carried out by the vicar, Robert Cremer, in 1747. While this concluded that the population was 3,213, by the time of the first official census in 1801 the population was 3,567. Of these, 2,307 lived in the main town area and the remainder, 1,260, in the surrounding rural area.

Agriculture

Britain as a whole was still in what has been called 'the Little Ice Age' which lasted from late mediaeval times until the late nineteenth century. This meant the weather was much more unpredictable and winters were sometimes severe, leading to poor harvests and food shortages. In November 1703 there was a Great Storm (similar to that of 1987) which badly affected all of Norfolk. Some years the winters were very bad, shortening the growing season and therefore affecting the harvest. Poor seasons and harvests affected everyone but especially the poor because of the scarcity of provisions, lack of work due to the weather and poor housing leading to deaths from extreme cold and disease. Parson Woodforde was the vicar of Weston Longville, a few miles north of Wymondham, and his diaries record several bad winters and storms in the latter part of the century, as in 1795 when he complained that the chamber pots froze.

Farming in Wymondham was typical of the claylands, with about half occupied by arable land, and half by meadows and pastures, although by the eighteenth century the emphasis was moving towards arable. There was growing use of turnips as winter fodder for cattle and clover also became more popular. This was used as fodder but also put nitrogen back into the soil, avoiding the need for any field to be kept fallow. Therefore, agriculture was made more economic and efficient. Farming included the fattening and dairying use of cattle which were sometimes grazed on the commons. The number of cattle kept in the area was reflected in the number of butchers, tanners and leather workers in the town. Although this area was on the claylands and therefore more suitable for cattle, sheep were also kept in considerable numbers and continued to be visible on the commons surrounding Wymondham throughout the century. In 1771 it was reported that *'Wymondham Common is an extensive waste terminated on all sides by trees etc. and covered with sheep'*.

The sheep were still present when Randall Burroughes (*see pp. 106-8 for biographical details*) was farming and keeping his farming journal in the 1790s. As one of the largest landowners in Wymondham, he had extensive common rights which he used for his sheep. For example, on Saturday, 30th July 1796 he wrote, *'The fat sheep on the common were examined every morning most frequently by myself a little after six'*. He also used the commons for his mares and colts, as on Friday 27th May 1796, when he recorded *'Whimsey her foal and two year old to Downham Common'* and on Saturday 30th July, when he noted *'one boy keeping sheep and colts on the common'*. Despite his use of the commons, he was certainly in favour of the move to enclose the remaining open fields and almost all of the commons in Wymondham, which began in 1806. During the eighteenth century, the view of commons in general had changed. The new ideas on cultivation were working against them and they were seen as useless 'waste' by many agricultural writers, as well as also acquiring a bad reputation associated with pauperism and crime. The Napoleonic Wars encouraged better use of land resulting in many Enclosure Acts, including that for Wymondham in 1806.

According to Mr Cremer's 1747 census, there were 120 families of gentlemen farmers *'and others'* (which presumably meant non-gentlemen farmers) in Wymondham, while there were 130 families of husbandmen and labourers, i.e. either smallholders or the labourers on all the farms. Although some skilled farm workers were employed full-time, such as shepherds or horsemen, others were employed on a day to day basis when needed, so income was not reliable. Wages for agricultural labourers were very low and between 1750 and 1800 wages went up by 25 per cent while the cost of living rose by 60 per cent, thus causing increasing hardship. A survey carried out in 1793 gave the following information for Wymondham: in 1752 labourers were earning 10d per day and one shilling in the summer. They also were given a dish of milk or broth in the morning and two pints of beer a day. By 1772 wages had increased to one shilling (12d) in the winter and 14d in summer, but not the milk or broth as previously. By 1792 they received 15d per day on average and one pint of beer, but no milk or broth. Over the same period the price of bread had increased far more so they were worse off. Bread was the stable food of the poor at this time (potatoes not yet being popular) so the price of corn was extremely important.

Trade

By the eighteenth century the market in Wymondham was held weekly on Fridays, while the fair was held three times a year, on February 2nd, May 6th and September 7th. The fair allowed traders from Norwich and elsewhere to bring goods not normally available in the town. It also sold livestock, as well as being the place for people, especially those working in agriculture, to change employers. There was also an element for fun: in the later part of the century the pauper children in the House of Industry in Wicklewood were allowed one penny each with which to attend the May fairs. The presence of the regular market and fairs should be remembered in the following description of the trades existing in Wymondham during the eighteenth century.

Mr Cremer's Census 1747

In 1747, besides counting heads in his unofficial census, Mr Cremer also noted the main occupations of the families. He did not break these figures into divisions so only the total for the parish are known. He was presumably counting only the main occupation of the head of the family and did not take any account of some men carrying out more than one trade, e.g. working on the land at times as well as weaving. It also does not reflect any trade carried on by other members of the household, such as the women working as spinners or servants, and journeymen or apprentices living in the household.

The figures given were:

Families

Gentlemen farmers & others about	120 (17.5%)
Husbandmen or labourers	130 (18.9%)
Weavers	155 (22.6%)
Alehouse keepers	39 (5.7%)
All other Trades, Businesses, Employments & Poor	242 (35.3%)
Total	**686**

From these figures it will be seen there was a large 'miscellaneous' group which must have covered shopkeepers, tradesmen such as blacksmiths etc. as well as surgeons, attorneys and brewers. Perhaps it also included the wood turners, who otherwise were not mentioned. Wymondham was well-known for its wood-turning but there is very little mention of this trade in the eighteenth-century records. The figures above certainly show the importance at this time of the weaving trade, of which more below.

Urban Wymondham from 1782 to 1788

Much more detail of the different trades in Wymondham can be obtained from a record kept in the 1780s by the vicar, Mr Peter Petit. He was trying to collect money for the church and kept a list of all the householders in the urban area including details of their trades. As the record only included the town itself, most of the biggest landowners were not included, and nor were most of the farm-workers. It only covered heads of households, so other workers living in the houses were not included, such as journeymen and apprentices, wives working at spinning, and also the live-in servants of the gentry and the better-off.

The list kept by Mr Petit embraces a wide range of social classes living in the town from professional men to paupers. Amongst the 'better sort' and the educated were gentlemen, attorneys, clergy, schoolmasters and surgeons. There were also wealthy tradesmen such as John Stephenson Cann who owned a local brewery and numerous public houses, but who was accepted as a gentleman by his peers.

There was a wide variety of food suppliers and retailers, including bakers, butchers, grocers and brewers. The large number of butchers reflected the number of cattle and sheep kept locally. There were also over twenty inns and taverns in the urban area alone. These varied from the large coaching inns to small ale-houses.

The many tradesmen included blacksmiths and wheelwrights, brickmakers, carpenters and masons. There were tanners and other leather workers using the hides from all those cattle.

The lone spindle-maker mentioned seems to be the only remnant of the town's wood-turning fame and was producing goods used in the textile trade. Earlier in the century, Blomefield, the Norfolk historian, stated that Wymondham was famous for the making of taps, spindles, spoons, and such like wooden ware in abundance. This trade must therefore have quickly deteriorated during this century. (However, there were still a few wood-turners around in 1836 as a wood-turner is shown in *White's Directory*, and the remnants of this trade probably resulted in the brush factories later).

The clothing trades were represented by dressmakers, tailors, stay makers, glovers and twelve shoemakers. There was also a watchmaker representing the luxury trades, but no doubt the better-off went to Norwich for many other luxuries.

However, the major industry in Wymondham was the textile trade.

The Textile Trade

The large number of hand-loom weavers shown in the 1780s list were heads of households, and the number does not reflect the journeymen and apprentices also working. In addition, the women of the households worked at spinning and the children helped from an early age. All of this work was controlled by rules laid down in Norwich. This also applies to the wool-combers. There were also linen weavers who worked with hemp in this area, not flax as in other parts of the country. Edward Durrant was a linen weaver working from a house in Vicar Street which he rented from the Town Lands Charity for many years.

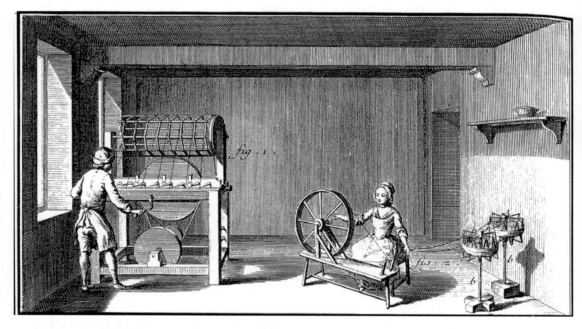

30. An eighteenth-century twisting mill plying yarn spun on the wheel. The workhouse set up in 1631 in Wymondham was equipped with a reconditioned 'twistering' mill of much the same design.

The textile industry was the main source of employment in the town at this time, as it had been for many years. In the first half of the eighteenth century, the textile trade in Norwich was thriving, mainly producing the fine Norwich 'stuffs' and worsteds, and this prosperity was spread though much of the county including Wymondham. As already stated, in 1747 Mr Cremer claimed there were 155 families of weavers in the parish, while in the 1780s there were 92 such families just in the urban area, so there may have been more in the country area. Many of these families must have included journeymen and apprentices apart from the head of the household. In addition, the women of the families were employed spinning the wool in preparation for weaving, and the children also worked. The whole trade was organised from Norwich with middlemen supplying the wool and collecting the finished article. This centralised administration had been in place since the Middle Ages in order to operate quality control. There were various Acts of Parliament passed regulating the industry in Norfolk to prevent *'abuses and frauds'* as well as to maintain the quality. Inspectors were appointed to visit the weavers establishments, which also enabled them to check on the quality of both the weaving and the spinners' work.

By the 1780s the Norfolk woollen trade was under growing competition from the West Riding of Yorkshire and the output of cotton in Lancashire was increasing. Cotton was lighter and easier to keep clean than wool. When the vicar, Peter Petit, listed all those trades mentioned above, he was attempting to collect money as Easter offerings from his parishioners. He was not very successful in these efforts, as many people were Dissenters, or just irreligious, or were short of money. It is noticeable that only three of the 92 weavers contributed. However, it is not clear if the others were Dissenters or simply could not afford to pay; quite possibly both were true. The weavers were scattered around the town, there being 31 in the Damgate area, 26 in Market Street, 19 in the Town Green and 16 in the Vicar Street areas. One of the linen weavers was in Town Green, the other in Vicar Street.

By the 1790s there was real hardship in the local weaving industry. The American market had already been lost due to the War of Independence in the 1770s. The war with France, which began in 1793 and continued almost continuously until 1815, cut off European export markets. In addition, the pressure from Yorkshire and Lancashire grew, partly by pursuing mechanisation, both of weaving and spinning, which the Norwich industry was unwilling to develop. During this period many women were prosecuted for 'false reeling', i.e. either embezzling wool provided for spinning or giving short lengths. For example, on 20th July 1805 it was reported twenty-four women were *severally convicted of false reeling and paid the penalty'*. These women often ended up in the Wymondham House of Correction (The Bridewell) if they were unable to pay the fine.

The trade continued into the nineteenth century but under increasing pressure, and became more centralized in Norwich itself as some mechanisation was introduced. By the 1820s, Wymondham was concentrating on the production of bombazines and crapes for mourning clothes and a small factory, run by Mr Cornelius Tipple, operated in Town Green in the old workhouse, where the Methodist church now stands.

Transport

Wymondham was on the main road between Thetford and Norwich, which developed as a major route from Anglo-Saxon times onwards, and which also became the main road to London via Newmarket in later times. By the eighteenth century, this was therefore one of the main routes between the first and second cities in the country.

The Highways Act (1555) which was still in force provided that two parishioners in every parish should be elected as Surveyors of the Highway. Every person with property over a certain amount was required to provide two labourers, equipment

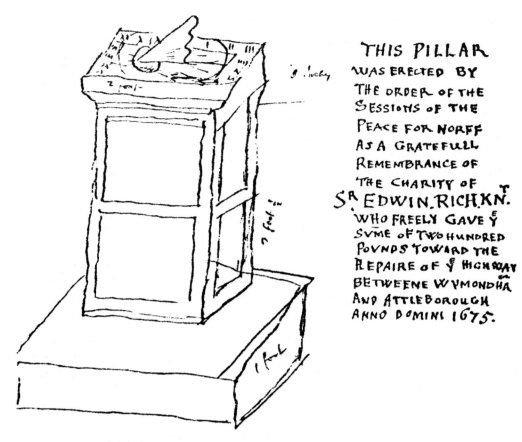

THIS PILLAR
WAS ERECTED BY
THE ORDER OF THE
SESSIONS OF THE
PEACE FOR NORFF
AS A GRATEFULL
REMEMBRANCE OF
THE CHARITY OF
Sᴿ EDWIN. RICH. KN.
WHO FREELY GAVE Yᵉ
SVME OF TWO HUNDRED
POVNDS TOWARD THE
REPAIRE OF Yᵉ HIGHWAY
BETWEENE WYMONDHᴬ
AND ATTLEBOROUGH
ANNO DOMINI 1675.

31. Memorial to the repair of the Wymondham to Attleborough 'causey'. Drawing of the Dial Stone from the notebook of Thomas Martin 1722.

and horses or oxen to repair the roads on four days a year. However, this Act imposed a heavy burden on those parishes, such as Wymondham, traversed by main roads.

During the seventeenth century, wheeled carts and wagons increasingly replaced packhorses and travel by coach also became more popular. This extra wheeled traffic caused even more wear and tear on the roads. In 1675 Sir Edwin Rich bequeathed £200 for the repair of the highway between Wymondham and Attleborough. The Dial Stone, which commemorates this gift, is still in place near the A11, although it had to be moved a few years ago when the Attleborough by-pass was built.

A new Turnpike Act in 1695 allowed a toll-road to be established between Wymondham and Attleborough after a new more direct route had been established between the two towns following the draining of Attleborough Mere. This was one of the earliest turnpikes in the country and certainly the first in Norfolk. In

1698 the diarist, Celia Fiennes, passed through Wymondham and recorded:

Thence I went to Windham a little market town, mostly on a Causey the country being low and moorish and the road on the Causey was in many places full of holes, tho' its secured by a bar at which passengers pay a penny a horse in order to the mending of the way, for all about is not to be rode on unless its a very dry summer.

Further stretches of turnpike were opened from Hethersett to Wymondham in 1708, and from Norwich to Hethersett in 1746–47. Before the latter though, a Turnpike Act in 1722 allowed the further extension of the turnpike in Attleborough. The Act gives the following reasons for this:

Great progress hath been made in repairing and amending [the road] . . . yet, by reason of the extraordinary decay of the said Roads, and the nature of the soil thereof, which is chiefly clay, . . . another part of the road not included [before] is, by means of the many heavy carriages daily passing through the same, become so very ruinous, that in some seasons of the year it is very dangerous to passengers, carriages, and cattle.

As was normal, this Act allowed surveyors to take gravel and other materials from the commons and wastes near the road without payment, but not from gardens etc. It also stated it was illegal to avoid paying the tolls by any *'Coach, Berlin, Chaise,*

32a. The Norwich mail coach in the mid-eighteenth century.

Chariot, Calash, Chair, Waggon, Cart, Carriage, Horse, or any other Beast or Cattle'. There were also fines for *'filth, dung, rubbish, watercourse drains, or other nuisances'* affecting the road. The references to cattle are a reminder that, apart from wheeled traffic, there was also considerable traffic from drovers taking herds of cattle to London. Animals being moved locally to new pasture were exempt from tolls, as, amongst, others were people attending church,.

MAIL COACHES

Passengers board at the White Horse, Fetter Lane London for each route at 7.30 p.m. each evening

Route 1 via NEWMARKET | Route 2 via IPSWICH

Miles	General Post Office	Down	Up	Miles	General Post Office	Down	Up
	London	8 p.m.	8 a.m.		London	8 p.m.	8 a.m.
18	Epping	10: 0	5:30	7	Ilford	9: 0	7: 0
7	Harlow	10:51	4:49	6	Romford	9:30	6:18
7	Hockerill	11:40	4: 0	6	Brentwood	10:20	5:27
12	Littlebury	1: 6	2:35	6	Ingatestone	11: 3	4:44
6	Bournbridge	1:50	1:40	6	Chelmsford	11:53	3:49
12	Newmarket	3:30	12:15	8	Witham	1: 3	2:44
9	Barton Mills	4:15	11:15	4	Kelvedon	1:38	2: 4
11	Thetford	5:30	9:30	10	Colchester	3: 3	12:39
9	Larlingford	7: 0	8:30	18	Ipswich	5:33	9:49
6	Attleburgh	7:50	7:45	12	Stonham	7:31	8:16
6	Wymondham	8:39	7: 0	12	Scole Inn	9:13	6:35
9	Norwich	10: 0	5:30	10	Long Stratton	10:30	5:20
22	Yarmouth	1 p.m.	3 p.m.	10	Norwich	12 Noon	4 p.m.

32b. London to Norwich mail coach timetable

As turnpike trusts proliferated throughout the eighteenth century, roads gradually improved encouraging traffic to increase, which in its turn brought new ideas, and the rapid spread of news. The choice of transport increased: mail coaches were the fastest, with four passengers inside and six outside. Stage-coaches were slower and carried more passengers. The first regular coach from Norwich to London began in 1762 and mail-coaches in 1785. By 1802 the Norwich Mail Coach Office was running coaches to London every day, one via Ipswich and one via Newmarket, which passed through Wymondham. A timetable of the period shows that the mail-coach leaving London mid-evening could reach Wymondham in under thirteen and Norwich within fourteen hours. Meanwhile, the wealthy could hire post-chaises for private use. Goods services also improved, with carriers providing regular services, both locally and long-distance to London. Passengers were taken, too, and this was the way that people travelled who could not afford

33. View from Damgate Bridge towards town centre. The Sun Inn on the right (now a private house) was a stopping place for carriers' carts, the cheapest passenger transport of their day.

the high charges of coaching companies. Ironically the golden age of this road traffic was the 1820s and 1830s, before it rapidly collapsed after the arrival of the railways in the 1840s.

Effect on Trade and the Town

The trade brought by the turnpike traffic would have been considerable. The blacksmiths, wheelwrights and waggon-makers would all have benefited. However, the main beneficiaries were the coaching inns. In Wymondham these were the King's Head, in the Market Place (where Woolworth's now stands), and the White Hart and the Griffin, both in Market Street. However, the King's Head was the most important, acting in some ways as the town community centre. It was already mentioned in seventeenth-century documents, but became important with the growth of the coaching trade. It was probably originally a timber-framed building but all pictures of it show it as having a Georgian brick facade. Many official meetings were held here, such as the Turnpike Commission mentioned above, and petty and quarter session for the Justices of the Peace (it was conveniently near the Bridewell!). Amongst others meeting there were the Directors of the Forehoe Incorporation, who after 1777 were running the House of Industry in Wicklewood. Auctions and sales were also held there. However, there were also more festive occasions, with assemblies, dinners and concerts. An early example was in 1712, when the trustees of the Town Lands Charity paid £2 to entertain the Cambridge scholar at the King's Head (In the sixteenth century, Matthew Parker, the Archbishop of Canterbury, had instituted a scholarship to Cambridge for a pupil from Wymondham). Later in the century frequent assemblies were held here. One example of an entertainment provided here was a concert and ball held in October 1774 and advertised in the *Norwich Mercury*.

From Attleborough the road ran up Damgate Street and round the sharp right-hand corner into Market Street, along to the Market Place and then down Bridewell Street towards Norwich. These streets are all narrow and there must sometimes have been complete confusion with coaches outside the inns and wagons, carts and carriages causing traffic jams.

In 1771 a prospectus was issued inviting application for shares in a scheme for the construction of a canal from Norwich via Wymondham, Hingham and Watton through to the River Ouse. Nothing seems to have come of this speculative venture.

Some eighteenth-century vicars

After the Toleration Act of 1689, Dissenters (but not Roman Catholics or Unitarians) were allowed to worship separately and no longer required to attend the parish church. However, they were all (including the Catholics etc.) still required to pay church rates and tithes which contributed to the maintenance of the vicar and church building and they were all excluded from holding any public office until 1828. By 1827 the vicar, Mr Papillon, reported that about 2,000 people, including children, attended the parish church, while about 1,500 attended the numerous nonconformist chapels. There were about 600 people (including their children) who failed to attend any place of worship due to age or infirmity. In addition about 900 others did not attend any church or chapel. (These figures make the population 5,000 at this time). Both the Dissenters and non-attenders were said by him to be tradesmen, farmers, weavers and husbandmen. There was also one family of Jews. Many people continued to attend the parish church and the vicar was always a leading member of the community.

During the eighteenth century there were a series of vicars who remained in this post for many years until their deaths. Amongst these was George Taylor who was vicar from 1701 until 1737. He also acted as temporary schoolmaster at the Grammar School in 1708 until a new one, Mark Pertt, was appointed early in 1709 by the trustees. However, Mr Pertt made himself unpopular very quickly for some unknown reason and at a town meeting of over eighty inhabitants the appointment was overturned and Mr Taylor re-appointed schoolmaster. He continued to carry out both his parochial and teaching duties until 1714 when a new schoolmaster was appointed.

The next vicar was Robert Cremer who held the post from 1737 until his death in 1768. It was he who carried out the very useful census in 1747 already mentioned above. At his death James Bentham was appointed but only remained a very short time. He was followed by Peter Petit, who remained in post until 1788. During the 1780s he kept a record of his attempts to collect Easter offerings around the town for the church. Judging from the amounts collected this was a thankless task, but it left an invaluable record of the trades operating in the town, as referred to above.

Mr Petit died in 1788 and was replaced by William Papillon. He was a young, energetic and wealthy man who had a great influence over various aspects of town life in the next forty-eight years, until he died in 1836. More details of his life appear on p. 109 below.

In 1793, a few years after Mr Papillon became vicar, a social event was held to celebrate a new organ in the church. Ann Farmer, *'a maiden lady of the parish'*, had left £630 for this instrument and an inaugural concert was held featuring a selection of sacred music performed before a *'genteel and numerous audience'*.

Organisation

The way the secular parish functioned had changed little since the seventeenth century, depending still on the vestry, manors and JPs working together. It appears, however, that the feoffees of the Town Lands Charity were now operating separately from the vestry, compared with the previous century when they seemed to be combined. In practice, there was an oligarchy of leading inhabitants, although in addition non-resident gentry such as the Wodehouse family in Kimberley and the Hobarts of Intwood, who both owned large amounts of land in Wymondham, had considerable influence in the town. (The Hobarts were lords of Grishaugh Manor and therefore responsible for the running of the market).

Poverty

The Overseers of the Poor (under the supervision of the JPs) were responsible for the care of the poor, collecting the poor rates and distributing the money as they thought fit. They also ran the workhouse in Town Green, which had been in operation since 1631. This had a population of forty-four persons in the summer of 1747, when Mr Cremer carried out his census. There was continuous discussion in the country about the best way to treat the poor, and continuous complaints about the cost of the poor rate. To those paying out this always seemed to be increasing, hence the severe rules about settlement, which forbade payment of relief to anyone not belonging to the parish. This led to arguments between parishes as to

34. Wicklewood House of Industry (later Union workhouse) built in 1777 for the Forehoe Incorporation.

responsibility for the poor person. One example of how the system worked can be seen in the case of Daniel Slight. In 1773 the parish of Hardingham paid two weavers settled in Wymondham, including Slight, to marry poor women from Hardingham. After marriage, responsibility lay with the husband's parish so Hardingham would no longer be responsible for these women. Later, Daniel Slight asked the overseers for relief for himself and his wife, but was refused. He appealed to one of the local JPs, Thomas Beevor of Hethel, who ordered that he should be paid. However, a few weeks later he absconded to Norwich leaving his wife to be supported by the parish overseers and she became an inhabitant of the workhouse.

From 1750s there was a new interest in building large workhouses, called Houses of Industry, in Suffolk and then Norfolk. These were based on the hundreds, that is the old groupings of parishes which acted as administrative groupings within the counties. The first such house in Norfolk was built at Heckingham in 1764 to cover the Loddon and Clavering hundreds. There was then a delay due to unrest caused by the dislike of this new form of poor relief, which imposed confinement and regimentation. However, by the 1770s the rising cost of poor relief renewed interest in the scheme and three more opened in 1777, including one at Wicklewood which covered Wymondham as well as the rest of the hundred of Forehoe. The others were at Gressenhall and Rollesby.

The House of Industry was run under an Act of Parliament as a corporation, which was responsible for all the centralised poor law in Forehoe, so the parish overseers now had a lesser role which involved reporting weekly to the committee who made the decisions. In theory all poor people asking for relief had to enter the House of Industry, where they had to work for their keep, either on the farm or at spinning and weaving. In practice, this did not work as some were only out of work for short periods and were needed, for example, as farm labourers at busy times of year. The majority of the inmates were the old, sick, widows, unmarried mothers and orphans. Although life in the House was not easy and was unpopular due to the regimentation involved, it did mean that people got three meals a day, clothing and medical attention if necessary. Families were not split up, as happened under the new Poor Law from 1834, and the children received some basic schooling.

The local charities also helped the poor. The long-standing and influential Town Lands Charity gave money at different times in this period. In addition Robert Dey had left money in 1672 for the apprenticing of poor children and in 1692 Ann Blackbourn left money for the poor, which was distributed at Christmas and Easter. In 1722 John Hendry left money for the poor as well as contributing to the local charity school. He also bequeathed money to pay the vicar for giving sermons every Sunday evening and every Friday in Lent.

Health

There were surgeons in Wymondham throughout the century, but there is no evidence of any physician working here. Surgeons were trained by apprenticeships, whereas the more expensive physicians had been to university. The surgeons in the 1780s were two James Carvers (father and son), plus Thomas Talbot. All three were well-off and involved in different aspects of town life and can be regarded as gentlemen as well as surgeons. Medicine was very basic at this time and there was a heavy reliance on blood-letting as a cure. Most people would have treated themselves whenever possible. Although the surgeons had to be paid, sometimes the Overseers of the Poor would pay for treatment of the poor. After the Forehoe Incorporation was set up in 1777, it paid for treatment, including home visits when necessary and the provision of medical aids such as wooden legs for amputees, trusses for hernias and inoculations for smallpox. The Norfolk and Norwich Hospital had opened in 1771, to which both the directors of the Forehoe Incorporation and the trustees of the Town Lands Charity subscribed, which allowed some of the poor to be sent there for treatment.

There is also evidence that an infirmary was built on the Lizard in 1767 which was probably for smallpox cases. This cost £206 to build and was paid for by the Town Lands Charity, but it is not clear how long it lasted. Otherwise, there were midwives (one was shown on the 1780s trade list discussed above) and probably untrained persons willing to act as tooth-pullers.

Education

The grammar school, which was run by the Town Lands Charity, had been in existence since the sixteenth century and was housed in Becket's Chapel. All its schoolmasters had Cambridge degrees and were ordained.

Besides the grammar school, there were other schools. There was at least one charity school teaching reading and writing to both boys and girls, which was subsidised after 1722 by Hendry's Charity. There may also have been other small schools or private tutors.

Law and Order

Justice in the eighteenth century continued to be harsh. Lesser crimes were dealt with by the JPs who met in the King's Head. They could condemn people to the stocks outside Becket's Chapel, where there was also a lock-up, or to the whipping post at the Market Cross. They could also sentence people to a period in the Bridewell, or House of Correction, which had opened in the early seventeenth century. In 1739 Blomefield, the Norfolk historian, referred to this as follows: *'Idleness, which this town seems to abhor, there having been a bridewell or house of correction for idle persons and such like, many ages, which is still kept in a house belonging to the county appropriated to that use'*. More serious crimes were heard at the assizes in Norwich and prisoners were kept in Norwich Castle. They could be hanged, or the sentence could be commuted to transportation to the colonies in America until their loss, and then to Australia. In 1712 two men, Robert Borrett and William Boughten, were hanged in the Market Place in Wymondham for the murder with robbery of a James Poynter. The gallows was built specially and cost £7 10s to erect. Their bodies were subsequently hung in chains on a gibbet along the Norwich Road, about a mile outside town. The vicar recorded that their bodies were still hanging there a year later.

In 1779 the Wymondham Bridewell was visited by the prison reformer, John Howard. He described the inmates as *'dirty and sickly objects at work with padlocks on their legs'*. The prison area consisted of a men's room to which were attached three small 'closets' for night rooms. There was a room reserved for women and there was also an underground dungeon. John Howard complained that the local magistrates had not obeyed a recent Act of Parliament and were still allowing prisoners to be kept in this dungeon when there was adequate accommodation elsewhere in the prison.

35. Wymondham Bridewell, the model prison built in the 1780s, which was run according to the principles of prison reformer, John Howard.

Following this poor report the local magistrates, headed by Sir Thomas Beevor, decided to rebuild and enlarge the prison along the lines recommended by John Howard. These included separate cells for each prisoner, with silence as the general rule. Men and women were kept apart and had their own exercise yards. The prisoners were also required to work for twelve hours a day. This enlarged bridewell with its individual cells became the model for new prisons in England, Wales and also America after 1785.

Buildings

At the end of the seventeenth century Wymondham was a town of timber-framed buildings, but in the next century this changed with the wide use of brick, including the Bridewell. The changes began with the rebuilding of some of the larger houses around the edges of the parish belonging to the gentry, such as Burfield and Kimberley Halls, then to the building of large town houses like Caius House in Middleton Street. By the end of the century there were also smaller houses, as can be seen in Vicar Street, and also new fashionable brick fronts had been added to the old timber-framed houses, as in the White Hart Inn and No. 1 Market Place. Some of these houses are listed below.

36. No. 1 Market Place: a three-storied timber-framed house cased in brick, one of only two in Wymondham. The other was the Yeoman's House in Town Green.

Burfield Hall

Built in 1709 by the Blackbourn family, this house was later owned by Samuel Denton, whose daughter, Jane, married Randall Burroughes in 1792. He already owned Browick Hall and considerable land in Wymondham. Burfield Hall became their home while Samuel's widow, Jane, moved to a new house in Wymondham itself (*see Fig. 40, p. 107*).

37. Cavick House, built in 1720.

Cavick House

This attractive house, just outside the town, was built in 1720 by John Drake and was sold in 1825 to local brewer, William Robert Cann.

Kimberley Hall

The large estate of Kimberley was the seat of the Wodehouse family from the Middle Ages, but in 1712 the fourth baronet, Sir John Wodehouse, built a new house in the park. This was enlarged by by Sir Armine Wodehouse, the fifth baronet, who added four corner towers *c*.1754. Two wings were added in 1835.

Stanfield Hall

This estate descended to the Jermy family in the eighteenth century, then to Isaac Preston through marriage. Before he died in 1796 the house was rebuilt in 1792 (*see Fig. 47, p.* 121) and was again altered in the 1830s for the Revd George Preston. His son, Isaac, took the family name, Jermy, and was murdered in 1848 in the notorious Rush murders.

14–16 Vicar Street

The eighteenth century part of this house, No. 16, was built by the new vicar, Revd William Papillon, in 1793 as he did not consider the vicarage to be satisfactory for his purposes. When he died in 1836, the house was purchased by John Mitchell, one of the town's leading attorneys. The house was extended (No.14) in 1880 by Mr. Pomeroy, the successor of Mr. Mitchell and Mr. Clarke (see below), and the

38. Caius House, Middleton Street, built by Jeremiah Burroughes in the 1740s.

extension was used as offices for the law firm.

Caius House
This large three-story town-house in Middleton Street was built in the 1740s by Jeremiah Burroughes, a local landowner (the grandfather of Randall Burroughes).

Abbotsford
This large house in Vicar Street was built about 1810 by the attorney, John Mitchell. He advanced his fortunes by marrying Martha, the daughter of the wealthy William Jackson, who lived at Wattlefield Hall, where John and Martha later lived and which they modernised in the 1820s. Mitchell's junior partner, Edward Palmer Clarke, also married well and lived in Abbotsford in the mid-nineteenth century, having purchased it from Mitchell in 1859. The legal firm's offices were based here until moving next door to Nos. 14–16.

Town Council Offices
This house in Middleton Street was built in 1792 by Randall Burroughes for his mother-in-law, Ann Denton.

39. Wymondham Town Council Offices, Middleton Street. Built by Randall Burroughes in 1792.

House Contents

Besides the houses themselves changing in style, they were also becoming more comfortable. An inventory of 1707 for the schoolmaster, Richard Clarke, shows he owned seven needlework chairs, as well as the usual wooden ones, and a couch. He also had a looking glass and a window curtain. He possessed a watch with a silver case and a collection of silver plate which included two cups, a tumbler and forty-two spoons. He also owned 240 books, a large number even for an educated man at that time. Later, in 1765, Robert Tungood's inventory shows more new items, including a walnut settee with cushion, a bureau, two tea tables and, sign of the times, six china cups and saucers.

The Napoleonic Wars (1793–1815)

During this period there was much hardship in Wymondham. The farmers were doing well because of inflation and the need for food for the armed services, but the farm workers wages were depressed and a gulf gradually grew between the employers and the employed. The weavers were also suffering due to the drop in trade and the challenge from the new weaving industries in Yorkshire and Lancashire. In addition, there were several bad winters in the 1790s.

The amount of outdoor relief paid out by the Forehoe Incorporation increased enormously in the 1790s, and the Town Lands Charity also paid money to many poor in Wymondham. The winter of 1794–95 was very bad and Randall Burroughes recorded in his diary that he, as a JP, had to intervene when a crowd were threatening a farmer who they insisted was hoarding corn. In 1800 the situation was so bad that the Town Lands Charity set up a soup kitchen which continued for three years. In 1801 the parish clerk of Forncett St Peter noted that there was a very bad fever in Wymondham as well as an outbreak of smallpox. Further, he stated that flour was 7s 6d a stone, the place was full of soldiers and the bells were always tolling for deaths. In addition to the daily problems caused by the economy during the 1790s and early 1800s, there were also fears of invasion by Napoleon for which the authorities had detailed plans to annex carts for evacuation.

The poor law records show a gradual improvement in the next few years. In 1806 the landowners started the procedure for enclosing the commons of Wymondham, but it is not clear whether this caused hardship for the poorer people of the town or provided much needed employment.

Randall Burroughes 1761–1817

At the time of the Commons Enclosure in Wymondham in 1810, Randall Burroughes was the biggest landowner in Wymondham and he is well-known because he kept a farming diary in the 1790s. He is included here as an example of a typical country gentleman of the times. He was born in 1761 and was the son of Diana and Jeremiah Burroughes. His grandfather, also Jeremiah, came from Norwich and made a good marriage to Ann Randall, the daughter of a wealthy Wymondham brewer, Thomas Randall. Jeremiah II also married well to Diana

Burkin of North Burlingham Hall, so by the time of Randall's birth the family was well-established, owning property both around North Burlingham and in Wymondham, including Browick Hall. Memorials to both Jeremiahs can be seen in Wymondham Abbey.

Randall's father died in 1767 when Randall was only a boy, so both he and his older brother, James, were brought up by his uncle, the Reverend Randall Burroughes of Long Stratton. Randall attended Emmanuel College, Cambridge, for a year in 1778, but then went to Lincoln's Inn in 1779.

Randall's older brother, James, had inherited most of their father's property, but Randall started farming in Suton and in 1790 the two brothers came to an arrangement about consolidating their properties. Randall acquired most of the lands in Wymondham, including Browick Hall, various public houses, farms,

40. *Burfield Hall, the home of Randall Burroughes at the end of the eighteenth century.*

cottages and land, while his brother concentrated on the property around North Burlingham.

Randall later purchased more properties and land, and he also made a good marriage, to Ann Denton, in 1792. She was the daughter of Jane Denton, the widow of Samuel Denton of Burfield Hall, and in the marriage settlement Randall acquired another 202 acres of land. He built a house in Wymondham for his mother-in-law, which is now the building containing the Town Council offices in Middleton Street, and in 1795 he and his wife moved into Burfield Hall.

The farming diary, which has been published by the Norfolk Record Society, was kept between 1794 and 1799. It shows Randall to have been a 'hands-on' gentleman farmer, who kept busy supervising activities on the farm. As was normal at the time, he operated mixed farming, with a mixture of arable and livestock farming, including sheep as well as cattle. As he was lord of Burfield Hall, Stalworthy and Nothes Manors, he had grazing rights on the commons surrounding Wymondham. He was commended by the agricultural writer, Arthur Young, for his *'good management'*.

In 1806 Randall, as a major landowner, was one of the leading lights in the move to enclose the commons. At that time he owned about 1,100 acres, much of which was let to tenants, and when the commons were enclosed and shared out by the Enclosure commissioners, he acquired another 227 acres.

In addition to his farming Randall also took his part in the other activities expected of gentlemen of the time. He was a Justice of the Peace, administering justice to the local miscreants at petty sessions held in the King's Head in Wymondham, and also attending the quarter sessions with his fellow JPs. He was a trustee of Buckenham Turnpike and was a deputy lieutenant of the county. As a director of the House of Industry in Wicklewood, he dealt with the poor of the whole of Forehoe Hundred. This was a period of great hardship for the poor due to inflation caused by the war with France and there was much unrest. His diary shows he was involved in confrontations with groups of paupers more than once.

Randall and his wife had four children: one son, Randall, and three daughters, Diana, Ann and Jemima. Diana married a Mr. Spinks, Ann remained unmarried and died in 1859. Jemima died much younger, aged twenty-two in 1820. Randall himself died, aged fifty-six, in 1817, leaving his property to his son. However, Randall (junior) also died unmarried in 1820 and left his property to his unmarried sister, Ann. Randall's wife, Ann, died in 1827.

Randall Burroughes' memorial tablet can be seen in Wymondham Abbey. It states that *'in private life he was kind, generous and sincere; in the discharge of his public duties intelligent and firm, at the same time mild and lenient: in every station his conduct was marked by a conscientious uprightness, which ensured the respect and esteem of all who knew him'*.

The Reverend William Papillon 1761–1836

William Papillon was vicar of Wymondham from 1788 (aged 27) until his death in 1836, the longest service of any of Wymondham's vicars.

William was the fourth son (born 1761) of a wealthy Kent family with Huguenot origins. Thus he had little expectation of prospects from his father, but in Wymondham he became a wealthy man by the shrewd purchase of properties and lands, giving him income from rents, and by an advantageous marriage to Sarah Martha Drake, the only daughter of the family which owned Cavick House. A life interest in Cavick House and its estate was settled on Sarah and William in her marriage settlement, and the couple made it their home until Sarah's early death in 1810. William advantageously sold his life interest for sufficient money to build himself a modern spacious home suitable to his needs at No. 16, Vicar Street. He never liked the vicarage, although he lived there until his marriage, and rented it to his curate.

William Papillon was a conventional clergyman of his time and believed the sermon to be an integral part of the church liturgy. In 1825 he arranged for a new pulpit to be installed in the nave for this purpose and new pews were also installed during his incumbency. (Both pulpit and pews have now gone). He was also concerned about services being disturbed by noise and traffic from the road from Vicar Street to Becket's Well which then ran much closer to the church. Therefore, in 1826 he applied – successfully – to have the route moved further away to its present line. There was also a suggestion in 1830 that the main turnpike road through Damgate be re-routed over Abbey Meadow. He successfully opposed that, saying he wished *'to keep the environs of the church from that state of desecration . . . even now liable... the service not being free from the noise of idle people on the outside'*.

Over the years William gradually purchased most of the land to the south of the church, including the ruined east tower, the chapter house arch and Abbey Meadow containing the remains of the dissolved abbey. In 1833 he set up the Papillon Trust which still owns these lands, and he therefore protected the view of the Abbey and its environs for the benefit of Wymondham until the present day.

During his incumbency, William set up a school (now the church offices), an infants' school in Lady Lane and also a Sunday school. These, too, were left under the protection of the Trust. In addition, the Trust was required to pay for a sermon to be given at the evening service.

William Papillon was vicar in Wymondham during a period of both international and local upheaval. The Napoleonic Wars were in progress between 1793 and 1815, incurring fears of invasion as well as the disruption caused by parishioners serving in the army or navy, or the local militia. In addition, this was a period of inflation and there was much hardship for the poor, exacerbated by the severe depression in the worsted weaving trade (the main local trade) and also several bad winters in the 1790s. William was a director of the Forehoe Incorporation, which ran the House of Industry at Wicklewood and administered the Poor Law throughout the Forehoe Hundred (including Wymondham). As a director he would have been intimately involved in the difficulties of the poor. He was also a feoffee (trustee) in the local Town Lands Charity which ran the grammar school and also helped the poor. No doubt William contributed to the aid of the poor in his lifetime and in his will he left £100 to be distributed to the poor of Wymondham.

William was living in Cavick House in 1806 when the parliamentary Act was passed for the enclosure of Wymondham's remaining open fields and almost all of the commons in Wymondham, which previously almost encircled the parish. By 1810 the appearance of the surrounding countryside had changed enormously, with many new hedged fields and straight-hedged roads. As a landowner he probably agreed with this action, considering it a much more effective use of land.

William Papillon died at his home in Vicar Street in 1836. He had no children, his wife had died many years before, and most of his estate was shared amongst relatives, apart from bequests to servants and the donation to the poor mentioned above. He was buried in the Abbey. He had been vicar for almost forty-eight years and his passing must have seemed like the end of an era to his parishioners.

CHAPTER SEVEN

The Nineteenth Century and to 1914

Early and mid-Nineteenth Century

The Enclosure of the Commons

The built up area of the town extended from the Bridewell to the Abbey and from Cock Street to the Fairland, and to Whitehorse Street. The rest of the parish was essentially rural and agricultural; but there were still extensive areas of commons around the outer areas of the parish with 'tongues' extending toward the town, particularly the Norwich Common which extended along the Norwich Road from the boundary with Hethersett to what is now Folly Road. There were extensive commons at Suton, Silfield and Downham, and smaller ones at Dykebeck and Browick. There were also some remnants of the old 'common fields', still held in strips, particularly the Northfield, north and south of Tuttles Lane.

The majority of the land was held by a small number of landowners. These included Henry Hobart, who owned the Park and other land in Silfield, Lord Wodehouse of Kimberley Hall with land in Downham, Randall Burroughes of Browick Hall and Burfield Hall, the vicar, William Papillon and William Jackson of Wattlefield Hall. Other landowners included King George III and Lord Byron. The large landowners were, with the lords of the various manors in the parish, the prime movers behind the Enclosure Act, which was a part of the national movement of the eighteenth and early nineteenth centuries to take into agricultural use the common lands that remained.

The procedure was to promote an Act of Parliament under which Commissioners were appointed who were charged with dividing up the commons and allocating the land to individual landowners in proportion to their claim for rights to use the common. Only owners of land and property could claim legal rights to use the commons; others who used the commons for grazing animals or to collect fuel only did so as a concession, not by right. The Wymondham Act was passed in 1806 and the only common excluded from enclosure was the Lizard. The Commissioners immediately began the process, first by putting an embargo on removing turf from the commons for fuel and then inviting claims. They received claims from over 200 people, including all the big landowners, small farmers who owned their land, and many of the owners of houses and commercial properties in the town. All claimed a right to graze cattle on the commons, some claimed the right to take fuel (in particular the owners of public houses) and the big landowners claimed the right of 'sheepwalk'.

Before the common lands could be allocated the Commissioners had to define the parish boundary – the first time this had ever been done accurately and with

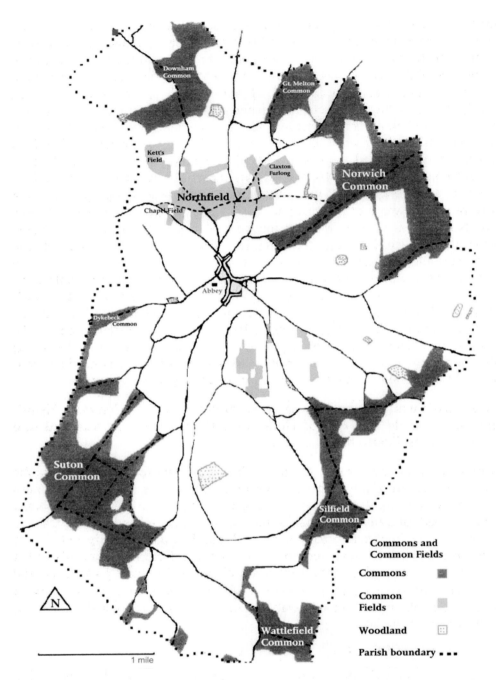

*41. Map of the pre-enclosure pattern of commons and common fields 1806.
A comparison with Fig. 15 shows that in the two centuries after 1600
considerable encroachment of both the commons and common fields had
occurred, while the woods had almost disappeared.*

authority – and set out new public roads across the common. Among the first allocations were plots to the Trustees for the Poor, which were intended to provide an income for the purchase of fuel for the poor who could no longer get fuel from the commons. After that the rest of the commons were divided up and awarded to those whose claims had been accepted. Many claims appear not to have been accepted, including the king's claim for sheepwalk, and with much dealing and exchange of land before the final settlement was made, the list of 'Awards' did not include over 100 of those who had made a claim. The big landowners and lords of the manors were awarded large areas: Randall Burroughes received 227 acres, Lord Wodehouse and William Jackson 137 acres each. Other landowners received awards in relation to the size of their ownership and 60 owners of properties in the town were given awards of a quarter or half an acre in plots along the north-east side of Norwich Road and on the opposite side beyond Spinks Lane. Suton common was divided up among the adjoining landowners with a pattern of new straight roads and three large plots awarded to the Poor's Trustees. The rent from these plots was intended to provide the income for fuel for the poor to replace the wood and furze that they had collected from the common. One of the new roads was Chepore Lane, apparently derived from the cynical nickname of 'Cheat-the-Poor'. There are few records to show the effect of the loss of the commons on the poor of Wymondham and initially the whole exercise would have provided work; but the long term effects must have been considerable, particularly on those who had used the common without legal right to graze a few geese or a cow.

The Commissioners also divided up what survived of the 'Common Fields', mainly the Northfield and north of Tuttles Lane to replace the old scattered strip holdings with consolidated blocks of land.

The Commissioners' awards had a lasting effect on the landscape. On most of the commons the pattern of the fields set out by the new owners followed the pattern of the awards [*see Fig. 43*]. However, along the north side of the Norwich Road from Folly Road for a mile and a half to the parish boundary and on the south side from Spinks Lane, in effect a long line of small building plots was created. These plots became the basis for scattered ribbon development from 1810 onwards with a concentration of early nineteenth-century development beyond Spinks Lane and the development of a small community which became known as Norwich Common. A public house, the Old Oak, was built in mid-century and a school in 1849 (the church came later).

The development of the town

Pigot's Directory of 1830 described Wymondham as *'a respectable town'* with a large Wednesday market for corn and three fairs, in February, May, and September, the last being for *'leanstock, horses, and pedlery'. Hunt's Directory* in 1850 still described the town as *'respectable'* but added *'and ancient'*, and

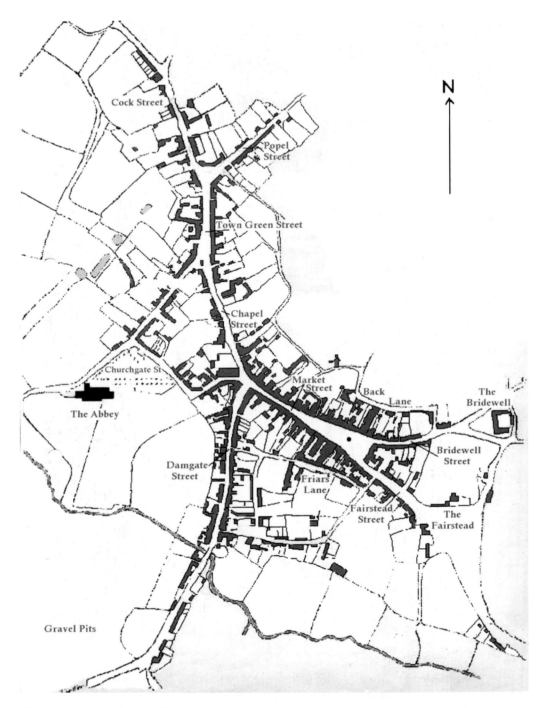

Cock Street

Popel Street

N

Town Green Street

Chapel Street

Churchgate St

Market Street

Back Lane

The Bridewell

The Abbey

Bridewell Street

Damgate Street

Friars Lane

Fairstead Street

The Fairstead

Gravel Pits

42. Map of the town of Wymondham taken from the Enclosure Awards map of 1810.

43. Suton and Spooner Row c.1890. The map shows the long, straight roads that were defined across the commons and the pattern of fields that followed the 'awards' of pieces of the common to the various landowners. Former areas of common are shown in white.

although *'decidedly antique'* was not *'entirely destitute of modern buildings'*.

Rather condescendingly it added, *'There are also a few good shops'*. It also referred to the three fairs but described the September fair as largely for *'pleasure and pedlery'*. The corn market was held on Fridays, but because it was dealt with by samples at the Griffin *'market day exhibits little of the activity and bustle usually manifested in other towns on market day'*.

One (unknown) writer in about 1849 referred to the building of the gas works, the railway station, the railway tavern and the cottages for railway workers as *'signs of*

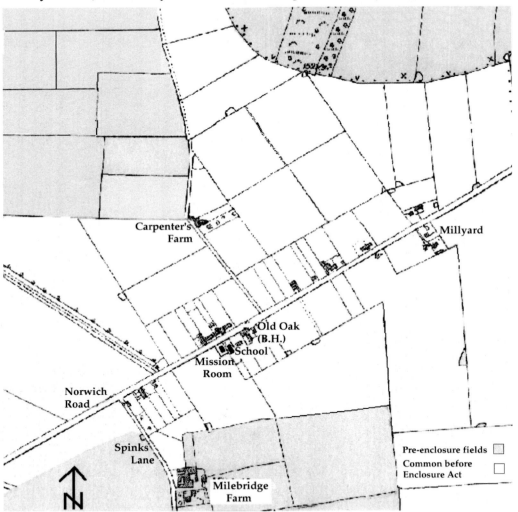

44. *The Norwich Common settlement in 1890. Small allotments of land awarded by the Enclosure Commissioners along Norwich Road were used as the base line for drawing up enclosure boundaries.*

vitality', but went on to contrast them to

> *the miserable rows of tumble-down dwellings occupied chiefly by the hand-loom weavers, whose shuttles may be heard with monotonous click-clack in their upper rooms . . . there are long rows of miserable houses almost destitute of furniture, and whose occupants in physical appearance are far inferior to the hardy sons of toil employed on the land. All round the town there are nests of these ruinous hovels presenting tier on tier of broken and patched windows, roofs with tiles blown off and no security against wind or rain. But beyond them may be seen many neat cottages and well cultivated allotments...*

The writer concluded, *'There are no intellectual amusements in this place, although it contains 5,000 people'.*

Later directories referred to the decline of the market; *White's* (1854) said, *'The market held every Friday is not numerously attended; corn is usually sold by samples at the Griffin Inn in the evening.'* In 1864 it blamed the new railway: *'The market held every Friday is almost extinct owing to the great facilities afforded by the railway for attending Norwich markets'.*

45. Northfield Mill which was erected in 1858 and burned down in 1950.

There were 4 windmills (Suton, Silfield, Northfield and Browick) producing flour. In 1830 there were the 3 coaching inns (the King's Head, the Griffin, and the White Hart) with 19 other taverns and public houses. In 1850 there were 26 inns and public houses listed.

117

The built-up area of the town did not expand significantly but there was considerable building and redevelopment in the town, including the creation of Queen Street and terrace housing at Bait Hill, Cemetery Lane, Norwich Road and other locations.

The Railways

Railway development came relatively late to Norfolk: the first railway in Norfolk opened in 1844 between Norwich and Yarmouth and the second, in 1845, between Brandon and Norwich, through Wymondham, as part of a new route to Cambridge and London. Wymondham station opened in 1845. The line was originally run by the Norfolk Railway, then taken over by Eastern Counties Railways in 1848, which was itself amalgamated into the Great Eastern Railway in 1862.

46. Wymondham Railway Station, which opened in 1845.

The branch line from Wymondham to Dereham began to take goods traffic in 1846 and passengers in 1847. It was extended to Fakenham in 1849 and Wells in 1857. A further branch line from Wymondham to Forncett on the main Norwich – Ipswich – London line opened in 1881.

The opening of the railway had both immediate and more long-term impacts on the local economy. The London to Norwich coaches which called at one of the Wymondham inns en route all stopped running within a year and the market declined as it was now so much easier to travel to Norwich.

A station at Spooner Row in the south of the parish also opened in 1845. A low number of passengers in the nineteenth century led to a series of closures and reopenings, services at times being limited to a Saturday train to and from

Norwich. There was also a very short-lived halt at Spinks Lane, which only appeared in the timetable for 1845 and may never have been used.

Administration

In the early years of the century the vestry remained the focus of local government, in some matters acting subject to the confirmation of the Justices of the Peace. It consisted of the vicar, (for many years William Papillon), the churchwardens, the overseers of the poor rate, and *'Principal Inhabitants'*. The official posts and others such as the constables and the surveyors of highways were all appointed by the vestry which also set the poor rate for poor relief, the Church rate, for the maintenance of the Abbey church, and the surveyors' rate, for the highways. It was also responsible for the fire engine which was kept at Becket's Chapel.

Law and Order

In 1820 there was a parish meeting which led to the setting up of the watch, funded by public subscription. Eight men were appointed constables, equipped with lanterns and rattles and charged with patrolling the parish from 7 p.m. to 5 a.m. *'The more respectable persons of the parish* [were to] *be requested to superintend such persons so to be employed.'* In 1821 the vestry considered the need *'for a proper place to make a cage to secure disorderly persons taken into custody by the watch'.*

There were oubreaks of rioting in Norfolk (and elsewhere) in 1830 and 1831 by farmworkers protesting about low wages and unemployment which they attributed to the introduction of new machinery, particularly threshing machines. Known as the 'Swing Riots', they focussed on the destruction of threshing machines and in Norfolk were concentrated in the north-east parishes and in south Norfolk between Wymondham and Diss. In November 1830 there were attacks in Wymondham on the police and the JPs, and some damage was done to property. After some attacks on the silk factories in Norwich in 1830, Jasper Howes Tipple, who owned the bombazine factory in Town Green, wrote to Lord Melbourne to say *'600 local weavers were ready to repulse the agricultural labourers if they enter the town'*. The vestry offered a reward *'to be paid on conviction of offenders in the late fires in this parish'.*

In 1833 the churchwardens were asked to convene another parish meeting to consider what needed to be done to provide for more efficent policing and lighting under new legislation, and 30 leading citizens undertook to superintend the nightly watch for the winter. The watchmen took an oath in the office of *'Constable'* to act as *'Watchman, Patrol or Streetkeeper'*.

In 1833 there was a case of arson at three farms in Wattlefield. Three men who were on parish relief were charged with setting fire to Mr Rix's stackyard. One,

Stephen Jackson, was reported to have said that he might as well do something to be hung for as to be starved. Their testimonies spoke of how they had to go to the House of Industry to collect their relief and of the weekly meetings they held, where, among other things, they read the Acts of Parliament which dealt with the remit of the Overseers of the Poor and collected subscriptions for a fund to help those in the workhouse. In their report on the fire, the *Norfolk Chronicle* said:

> *Wymondham has been for some weeks in a state of excitement occasioned as it is said by some recent alteration in the regulations for the poor and although there have never been fires here before three policemen have been sent for and have been in the town a fortnight or three weeks; this it seems has given great offence to the people and meetings have been lately held (some clandestinely and some openly) amongst the working people respecting these matters.*

In 1834 one of the churchwardens was sent a notice which warned him that a number of fireballs had been set into the roof of the church by *'numbers of men who are starveing for want of employ'*. They claimed that the farmers had the work but not the wherewithall to pay them. This was because they had to pay the parish rate, which included the police, and the wages of the police would pay for eleven men's work.

In May 1834 the *Norwich Mercury* reported that the hand-loom weavers of Wymondham had petioned Parliament for legislation *'for their relief'*.

The local gentry set up 'The Wymondham Association' under the presidency of Lord Wodehouse which offered rewards for information on local crimes and *'for promoting and rewarding good conduct and encouraging industrious habits amongst cottagers, labourers and servants'*. For example, sums of money were offered to girls who could demonstrate long service and *'irreproachable character'*, to the ploughman who could plough the straightest furrow and to the cottager who could grow the best onions.

The Bridewell closed for a spell from 1827 to 1832, when it became a prison for females (on average about 20 at a time) who were responsible for washing and sewing clothes for the men in Norwich prison.

Local murders

There were several murders which achieved a significant notoriety. In July 1841 John Self, aged twenty, was found guilty of the murder of Jemima Stimpson, who was 15, at Norwich Common. He had struck her on the head with a spade and thrown her into a pond. He was executed at Norwich Castle in August of the same year.

Stanfield Hall was the scene of a notorious double murder in 1849, when the owner-resident, Isaac Jermy, who was the Recorder of Norwich, and his son were shot by an intruder. The latter also fired at and wounded the son's wife and one of the servants before escaping. Suspicion fell on James Blomefield Rush, Jermy's bailiff, who lived at Potash Farm, about a mile from the Hall, whose relations with the Jermys were known to have been strained. Rush always maintained his innocence and he conducted his own defence at the trial which attracted widespread interest. His closing address lasted fourteen hours but, with the

47. Stanfield Hall, scene of the Rush Murders in 1849.

retraction of support for his alibi by his mistress, he was found guilty. He was hanged outside Norwich Castle in front of a very large crowd, one of the last public executions in the county.

In 1877 there was a double murder at 'The Rothbury' on Hewitts Lane, the residence of Thomas Mays, *'over 70 but hale and hearty and much respected by the townsmen'.* He had been a veterinary surgeon, but now ran a smithy, where he employed fifty-six year old Henry Bidewell and Henry March who was fifty-nine. March, who also ran a little shop with his wife where they lived in Pople Street, had worked for Mays for thirty-four years but they had fallen out. March and Bidewell had an argument in the smithy and a maid in the house saw March bludgeon Bidewell with an iron bar. Mays went to investigate and March hit him as well. Both men were so seriously injured that they died soon after. March walked down the road to the Feathers, had a pint of beer, then went home where he was arrested. He made a full confession, his only defence being that his actions were not premeditated.

He was tried, found guilty and hanged at Norwich Castle. A collection was made for the widows of both Bidewell and March.

Employment and Industry

The weaving industry continued into the nineteenth century. In the 1830s as well as Cornelius Tipple's bombazine factory in Town Green, there were also weaving factories in Friarscroft Lane (weaving horsehair) and off Damgate Street.

However, by the end of the 1830s the whole handloom industry was in crisis and a government commission reported that it was in a depressed condition throughout the whole country. In the 1840 Report from Assistant Commissioners on the Handloom Industry it was stated that the weavers in Wymondham constituted about one sixth of the male population. There were said to be about 300 looms, of which about 100 were employed by Mr Tipple in his bombazine factory. One of the local weavers reported: *'A parent tries to get his boy to anything rather than to weaving. There are no boys learning to weave now, nor have been for some time past. Anything is better than weaving. Some boys have taken to agricultural employment'*. In *White's Trade Directory* of 1845 it was reported that ten years before there had been six hundred looms in Wymondham but there were now fewer than sixty.

Nevertheless, the situation may not have been quite so bad as painted because the 1851 census still showed 336 weavers and associated workers in the town. In 1902 it was reported in the local paper that a weaver, James Ball, who had recently died in Wymondham, had exhibited a silk shawl which won a prize at the Great Exhibition in 1851.

As the century progressed, the textile industry continued to decline and by 1871 the number of weavers recorded in the census was 132 and in 1881 only 23. Some elements of the industry, including the horsehair factory (then R. B. Hovell's), survived to the early twentieth century.

The wood turning industry also declined and *White's Directory* in 1836 said Wymondham was *'once celebrated for spindles, spoons and other turnery ware but the industry is now nearly obsolete'*. However, Robert Semmence had the appropriate skills and eventually established sawmills and a turnery at Cavick, producing domestic ware and specialising in brush backs.

There was a tannery in Town Green which was in operation from the middle of the seventeenth century until the 1820s, when first William Browne and then his son

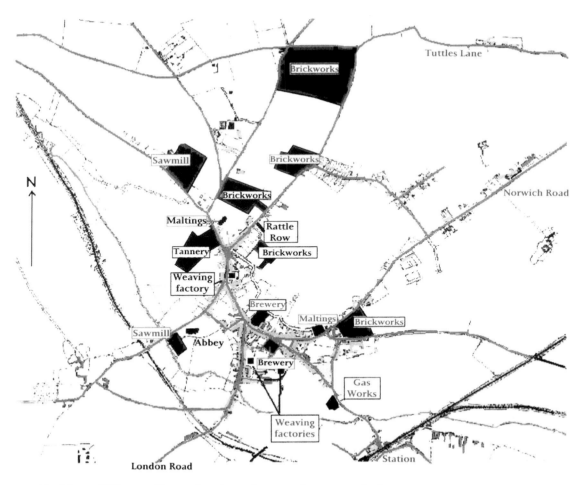

48. Map of Wymondham showing nineteenth-century industries.

Thomas became bankrupt. The premises (on the site of Applegarth) included drying sheds, weighing barn, beam house, bark house, tanning pits and offices, and used horse hides from Spain as well as local hides and skins.

Although several houses brewed beer, there were two sizeable commercial breweries, both in Market Street. The major one was on the south side, between Market Street and Brewery Lane: it became Cann's in 1780 and Cann and Clarke's in 1824. The business expanded and in 1832 acquired the second Market Street brewery, Harvey's. It became the centre of an extensive concern, owning 100 public houses from west Norfolk to Great Yarmouth in 1891. The business was sold to Morgan's of Norwich in 1894, but the premises in Brewery Lane were sold to S. D. Page and Sons, a brush-making firm, in 1896. The workers included maltsters, draymen, coopers, clerical staff and labourers, with over 20 brewery workers recorded in the 1851 census.

There were several brick kilns using local clays throughout the nineteenth century to produce a range of products, mainly red and white bricks, roof tiles and pantiles, but also pavement blocks, drains and clay lump. Brickworks at Norwich Road (opposite the Windmill public house) and at Hewitts Lane were run from the late eighteenth century until the 1820s by Thomas C. Watson senior and his son. In 1813 the firm produced over 300,000 bricks and 100,000 tiles, and maintained that rate of production to 1826–27. Individual workers were recorded making 70,000–80,000 bricks and 30,000–40,000 tiles in a year. In 1826 John Green made 116,700 red bricks, half the firm's production for the year. The Norwich Road site finally closed, as Sharpe's, in 1900 and the drying sheds were demolished by a crowd celebrating the relief of Mafeking. There was a brickworks between Melton Road and Pople Street (in the early years of the century, Harvey's) and another at the junction of Pople Street and Hewitts Lane. Both survived into the twentieth century, with the last, Bidewell's, closing in 1937.

The Wymondham Gas and Coke company set up its works at Station Road in 1848 and supplied gas for the street lights.

49. Becket's Chapel after restoration in the 1870s. It was used by the grammar school until 1903.

In 1841 37% of the workforce were employed in some form of agriculture, including 98 farmers. The occupations listed in the directories provided for all the basic needs of the residents of the town and its neighbourhood, with numbers of butchers (17 in 1841), bakers (9), grocers, boot and shoemakers, glovers (and breeches makers) and 2 straw-hat makers in 1850. There were craft trades such as carpenters, painters, plumbers, 3 cabinet and chair makers and trades like blacksmiths (23 in 1841) , wheelwrights (10 in 1841) and saddlers serving the farms, the carriers and all those with some form of horse transport

Churches (see earlier section on Nonconformity)

The Schools

The Grammar school functioned throughout the century, in Becket's Chapel and, from 1835 to 1888, in a house in Middleton Street (still identifiable by a plaque and the fleur de lys over the doorway). In the early years of the century there were at least three 'charity' schools and in 1834 the Vicar, William Papillon, started two National schools, at Church Street ,which had 155 children in 1864, and Lady's Lane (for infants). There were 'private' schools in Bridewell Street and a National school was built on Norwich Common in 1849. The first Nonconformist British school was opened next to the Independent (Congregational) chapel by the Fairland in 1848, lasting until 1863, and there was a 'Commercial School' at the Rothbury from 1886 to 1898.

Late Victorian and Edwardian Wymondham

Local Government

Towards the end of the nineteenth century the town began to see new developments and improvements that reflected changes in both national government and, particularly, in the shape of local government. The Forehoe Rural District Council (RDC), which included the parish of Wymondham, was established under the Local Government Act 1888. The Wymondham Parish Council met for the first time on 1st January 1895, electing Mr E. W. Routh Clarke as chairman and appointing Charles Robert Ayton as the clerk. The election of the vice-chairman was a fight between Mr Fryer and Mr Parry, a reflection of the division between Church of England and Nonconformists, which was a feature of political affairs throughout this period. Fryer, a churchman, won by 6 votes to 5. The issues of concern included the ownership and management of the Market Place and the Fairland (both then owned by the Hobart family as lords of the manor), the appointment of constables and overseers, the management of the cemetery and the Fire Brigade. There were also more mundane (but very necessary) matters like street watering and night soil collection. The latter was a particular matter of concern throughout the period until mains sewerage was provided in 1933.

One of the issues for the council in the period before the first World War was the *'Provision of Houses for the Working Classes'*. In the 1890s the council distributed a handbill to try and identify those in regular work and unable to hire

CAVICK ROAD. WYMONDHAM

50. Wymondham Abbey viewed from the south-west.

houses. There were eight replies but as the respondents *'only wanted to upgrade their accommodation'* the council decided to take no action. In 1914 the Forehoe Rural District Council considered there was a serious need for working class houses and was critical of the Parish Council's approach, but the Parish Council decided that there was no immediate necessity for council housing because *'private enterprise has been and will be forthcoming to meet the need'*. The rider to this conclusion reveals their attitude: *'if rate-aided houses are erected it will be the means of destroying local public spirit as far as building operations are concerned and will materially increase the rates of the parish'*.

In 1897 a proposal by a private company to provide a mains water supply to most of the town was a major cause of concern, mainly because it was perceived as a way of making people pay for what they then got 'free', from wells and pumps. The company promoted a private bill in Parliament but the Parish and District Councils organised strong opposition and the local MPs succeeded in having the bill thrown out at the First Reading, a very unusual occurrence, especially as the bill was supported by the Local Government Board. The result was hailed in the local press as a triumph for local democracy over big business but the problems of an inadequate water supply, especially for fighting fires, became increasingly serious.

Schools

The Wymondham School Board was established in 1872 and the Board schools in

*51. Local patriotism: a terracotta plaque celebrating Queen
Victoria's Jubilee (1887) in Church Street.*

Browick Road, with separate accommodation for boys, girls and infants, were opened in 1876, after Spooner Row in 1874 and Silfield in 1876. The school on Norwich Common was taken over in 1874. The Norwich Common community continued to develop with the opening of St Edmund's church in 1892. The Grammar School continued to function in various buildings in Middleton Street, including the Priory and York House, until 1888 and then in Becket's Chapel till it closed in 1903. The Commercial School was set up next to the Congregational Church on the Fairland in 1886, with about 100 pupils. It closed in 1898 after moving to The Rothbury in Pople Street.

The Fire Brigade

Fire engines were funded by the Town Lands Charity in the eighteenth century, and in the nineteenth century were maintained by the vestry until 1882, when the fire brigade was set up, funded initially by local subscription. The new fire station in Market Street was given by Mrs J. de B. Clarke. (The horse-drawn engine was still in use in 1935, although then towed by a lorry.) There were a number of spectacular and major fires in the period before 1914, including those at Browick Hall (1886), Kimberley Hall (1899), S. D. Page's factory and both sawmills. Perhaps the most devastating was the fire at Parker's Store in the middle of Market Street in 1901, when the shop, then the biggest in the town, was totally destroyed. Water supply was a serious problem at all these fires, except at the Cavick sawmills which were close to the river.

Employment and Industry

The timber related industries continued to be important, with the Semmence sawmills at Cavick run by Robert's son Albert after 1893, when his brother George set up the new Poynt sawmills at Melton Road. Both sites were subject to devastating fires; Cavick in 1907 and Melton Road in 1914. S. D. Page, brush makers in Norwich, established a new factory in Lady's Lane in 1890, producing, for the first time, machine-made brushes. Despite serious fires in 1890 and 1894 the firm expanded and acquired part of the old brewery in Brewery Lane (1896) as a factory for processing bass and fibres for the main factory. In 1900 the firm employed over 500 workers, including 200 at Wymondham, and produced thousands of various sorts of brushes per week. The private rail siding was opened in 1916.

Gravel production became increasingly important before and after 1900 to meet demands from the new highway authorities. Wymondham gravel included hoggin with a binding clay constituent which made it particularly suitable for roadworks and large gravel pits were opened up in Browick Road and at Silfield, mostly by the firm of C. R. Ayton. Up to 1914 about 200 men were employed by the firm and at peak times 40 to 50 truck loads of gravel were sent out daily, mainly to councils throughout the eastern region.

However, the varying fortunes of the working population continued throughout the century and a petition in the 1880s with 44 signatures, signed as *'The Unemployed of Wymondham'*, gives some insight into the hardships experienced by the less fortunate. It said, *'That through want of employment we and our families are brought to a state of destitution and in some instances to the point of starvation. We do not ask for charity nor for parish relief so much as for employment, we would much rather work for our bread . . . '* and concluded *'we earnestly pray you to devise some means for our assistance preferring honest labour to any other mode . . . '.*

Social Life

This was a period of varied social activity and new initiatives included the establishment of a private company, funded by local subscription, to build and run a town hall as a venue for concerts, shows and meetings. The Hall was opened in Town Green in 1890. Another initiative, just before and after the turn of the century, was the organisation by the Wymondham Sports Committee of a Whitsun Sports event, which became a major item in the town's calendar until 1909 and one of the most important and popular sporting occasions in the eastern counties. The Sports attracted large crowds to the town, with concessions for rail travellers and special trains from all over the country.

52. The Town Hall, Town Green. Built in the 1890s as an assembly hall, by 1931, when this photograph was taken, it was in use as a cinema.

One of the records of activities in the town is the diary of Henry Cushing, who ran a newsagents, and a furniture and china shop in Market Street. He was also a keen photographer and his photographs provide a fascinating record of the town and its residents. His descriptions of the Sports Days paint a colourful picture. In 1892 he wrote,

> *Town all alive. Preparations made everywhere. Club at Griffin taking up boughs and flags. Talbot went with Jack to the Sports, largest number there there had ever been. Labourers Union had a dinner and*

ball at Three Feathers. Grand Temperance demonstration . . . . We went to the Market Hill to hear the 'Blind Woman' sing, had to speak out to the Salvation Army lasses, they made an effort to surround the woman and hustle her off but we would not allow them – the town during the day was remarkably orderly. I only heard of one fight and that was between two women. For some reason the Congregational Temperance party took no part in it.

The next year, however, he wrote,

A tremendous lot of folks poured into the town for the sports – never saw so many folks at one before, nor so much drunkenness . . . . At night the place was perfect pandemonium, was glad enough when we had to close.

The Wymondham Agricultural Society ran an Agricultural Show for several years before the First World War, on the field in Norwich Road, known as the Showground, now occupied by the High School.

Very active as a town function was the company of Volunteers, the fore-runner of the Territorial Army. The Wymondham company ('F' Company of the 4th Battalion of the Norfolk Regiment) had its own brass band and paraded through the town every week. Several of the company volunteered to serve in the second Boer

53. Sports Day c.1900

War and their return was the signal for celebrations, as were the major events of the war, such as the relief of Mafeking and the fall of Pretoria. In addition to the organised celebrations, which included sports and processions through the town, there was more unofficial activity which included, in 1900, breaking up Sharpe's tile sheds as part of the celebrations.

Political life was coloured by the antagonism between the established Church and the Nonconformists on local issues. One example was the County Council election of 1913, when the opposing candidates were William Fryer, a local landowner, and the Reverend Edwin Russell, a Methodist minister. Both were prominent in town affairs and the election was marked by bitter accusations and counter accusations by their supporters.

Events such as the Royal Jubilees, Boer War triumphs and Coronations in 1901 and 1911, were celebrated with enthusiasm, and marked with town decorations,

54. The decorated arch erected to welcome King Edward VII when he passed through Wymondham on his way to Norwich in 1909.

sports, processions and teas. Particular excitement was aroused in October 1909 when King Edward VII drove through the town on his way to Norwich. Crowds lined Market Street, where a large decorated arch had been constructed, and the schoolchildren were assembled with the crowds on the Market Place.

The 1912 Floods

It had rained for three days before Monday, 26 August 1912, but then it started to rain heavily. In the next 30 hours over 7 inches of rain were recorded over much of East Norfolk and there was widespread flooding. The Tiffey and Bays rivers were described as *'raging torrents'* and the Cavick, Damgate and Station Road Bridges were all seriously damaged. Two cottages beside Damgate Bridge, occupied by the Hubbard and Nicholls families, were swept away and there was serious flooding in the town. All rail connections to Norwich were cut and trains were stopped overnight at Wymondham.

After the water receded, a parish meeting decided to set up a relief fund to help householders affected by the flood and the relief committee immediately gave two hundredweight of coal to between sixty and seventy cottages that were affected. The County Council also set up a committee which received claims for losses incurred, including over fifty relating to flooded cottages. There were 10 claims from Pople Street (where the water was *'2ft 7ins deep in the lower rooms'*), 8 from Norwich Road and Spinks Lane, 6 from Damgate Street, 3 from Love Lane,

55. Floods of 1912 at Damgate Bridge where the Tiffey destroyed two cottages.

and 1 or 2 from Chapel Bell, Back Lane, Station Road, the Lizard, Browick, Dykebeck, Spooner Row, Silfield, Suton and Carleton Bridge. The two cottages lost in Damgate Street received payment for all their furniture and household goods, and their claims provide an insight into the belongings of families in relatively humble circumstances. Nicholls was granted £5 for all his possessions, Hubbard £4. Most of the other claims in the town related to floor coverings, wallpapering, furniture, food and livestock (chickens and rabbits). The outlying claims related to crops destroyed and livestock lost. Local subscriptions were sufficient to meet the claims that were allowed, the majority in full.

Charles Robert Ayton

Charles Ayton was born in 1858. His father, who was the landlord of the Green Dragon and had a small farm, died in 1875 and his mother started an off-licence in Church Street. When he was twelve years old, Charles started work as a solicitor's clerk with the firm of Pomeroy and White. During the 1880s and 1890s he took on a number of posts, including Clerk to the Surveyors of Highways, and from 1880 to 1912 the Assistant Overseer to the Poor's Rate Collectors. He was the secretary to the Gas Light and Coke Company, secretary to the Grammar School Trustees and in 1898 became the first secretary to the new Public Hall Company. He was secretary to the Sports Committee from 1893 to 1905, when Wymondham Sports became one of the important sporting events in the region. On three occasions Charles was given presentations of purses of gold sovereigns and a gold watch for his efforts. He was also secretary to the Cricket Club and to the Cycling Club. He became a founder member of the new Fire Brigade in 1882 and about the same time he joined the Norfolk Volunteers (F company, based in Wymondham). He rose through the ranks eventually to become a major and the battalion quartermaster. The high spot of this career was the occasion on which the officers of the battalion dined with King Edward VII when he visited Norwich in 1909. He was in demand as a singer of comic songs and ballads at concerts and dinners, performing with the Wymondham Amateur Minstrel Troupe and the Norwich City Amateur Minstrels.

In 1895 he became the first clerk to the new Parish Council, and he was also clerk to the annual parish meeting and secretary to the Burial Committee responsible for running the new cemetery which opened in 1882. Following unseemly conduct at certain funerals he was instructed to display a notice to say that *'Perambulators will not be allowed on the cemetery when funerals are taking place'*.

He was secretary to the Coronation Committee organising celebrations at the coronation of Edward VII in 1902.

Around 1900 he bought land off Browick Road and started a company with four men and two tumbrels producing gravel for roadworks. The firm grew until it was employing over 200 men and sending 40 truck loads of gravel daily to highway authorities all over the east of England. Wymondham gravel was particularly noted for its clay content which made it particularly suitable for road-making.

In 1912 Charles Ayton resigned as clerk to the Parish Council and his commission in the Volunteers to give more time to the gravel business. Nevertheless he stood for the Parish Council and was top of the poll at the election. He served on the council till 1922, his last contribution being a study of the implications of the town becoming an Urban District, during which he visited other towns in Norfolk and Suffolk that had that status.

56. Victorian exuberance in Wymondham.

A doorway influenced by the Orient.

Ceramic medallion and string course.

A butcher's opulent, tiled frontage, of which there are several examples in Wymondham.

During the First World War he made himself and his office available, particularly to wives of serving men, to help with advice and in contacting service authorities. After the war, he played a major role in setting up the ex-servicemen's organisations and was the first president of the Ex-Servicemen's Club. He was active in the unsuccessful campaign to achieve a war memorial in the form of a tangible community facility (and not only a monument).

He was involved with the Oddfellows as a trustee, the Freemasons and, in his later years, the Conservative and Unionist Party, having left the Liberals over Irish Home Rule. In addition to the substantial areas of land acquired for gravel working, he bought other properties in the town in Church Street, Damgate Street, Avenue Road, Silfield, the Tithe Barn farm and the field known as 'The Showground' on Norwich Road. He left the latter to the town as a sports field but it was acquired by the County Council for the 'new' Senior School in 1935.

When he died in 1928 the *Eastern Daily Press* said he had been *'a prominent and popular figure in all the activities of the Town . . . and throughout his long life he enjoyed the confidence and esteem of his fellow townsmen and few men were more generally admired. A big tall man he was a striking personality in whatever society he moved and his affability and generous disposition brought him a host of friends'.* At his funeral, which was semi-military with the coffin on a gun carriage draped with a Union Jack, *'Business was almost suspended and large crowds of sympathetic spectators watched the passage of the cortege'.*

CHAPTER EIGHT

World War I & the Twentieth Century

The First World War

At the outbreak of war in 1914 many men volunteered for the army and the Territorials were mobilised, including the Wymondham company of the 4th Norfolks, many of whom served in Gallipoli in 1915, and later elsewhere in the Middle East. One of the men involved there, Pat Hurrell, left a written record of their experiences. Others served in the various theatres of the war and among the decorations awarded for gallantry in France were a Victoria Cross to Company Sergeant-Major Harry Daniels, the son of a baker in Market Street, and a Military Cross to Lieutenant Malcolm Ayton.

In 1914 a Red Cross Voluntary Aid Detachment (VAD) hospital for wounded servicemen was set up in Church Street and later the next year it was moved to part of Abbotsford, the home of Captain and Mrs Cautley. It had one ward and a day room, and the commandant was the vicar's wife, Mrs Rose Martin Jones. By the end of the war 73 nurses had worked at the hospital and over 800 patients had been treated. The hospital was supported by government grants and by local fund raising, which included concerts at the Town Hall, some including patients and staff.

57. A military funeral in the Abbey churchyard during the First World War.

The Parish Council were concerned at the possibility of air raids and resolved that in the event of a raid the fire brigade should not leave the parish. A lone Zeppelin is reported to have dropped a bomb at Silfield and there were also reports of Zepplins over the railway line at Dereham where some damage was done. Page's were kept busy and made over four million brushes for the services.

The Armistice was signed in November 1918 just as Wymondham was holding a 'Feed the Guns Week' to raise funds for the war effort. The peace celebrations included a procession, concert and dance, and a service of thanksgiving at the Abbey church. Events were organised with entertainments and dances to 'welcome home' returning servicemen. 'Peace Celebration' Day in July 1919 included a dinner for ex-servicemen, after childrens' events on the Fairland, sports on the King's Head Meadow, dancing and fireworks.

By the end of the war 142 Wymondham men had died on active service and over 400 had been wounded.

The town, in common with virtually every community, was concerned to ensure the remembrance of those who had died and there was some controversy as to the most appropriate memorial. Some favoured the dedication of the new reredos in the Abbey while others wanted a memorial in the town, or a community hall or recreation ground. The memorial monument was finally unveiled by Major Cautley in Town Green on the 24th July, 1921. Organisations such as the British Legion and the Ex-Servicemen's Club were established and became part of the

58. The War Memorial at Town Green in the 1920s.

town's social life.

The Inter-War Years

The Development of the Towns

One issue of major concern was the aim to achieve Urban District Council (UDC) status for the town, which would give the Town Council a much more direct control over its administration and services. The Parish Council led a long campaign to this end, but initially the County Council would not accept the whole parish as appropriate for Urban District status and it was not until 1935 that Urban District status was achieved. The Parish Council put together an account of the town in 1921 to support their case, referring to the size of the parish and its population of 4,814. They stated that Wymondham's attributes included a gasworks, a fire brigade (with two engines), a police station (a superintendent, a sergeant, and two police constables), 12 churches and chapels, 4 public elementary schools, the Public Hall, the Great Eastern Railway stations at Station Road and Spooner Row, a motor bus service to Norwich, brush factories, stone pits and timber sawmills. Among their concerns were the lack of a mains water supply and mains drainage. The town was still relying for its water on wells and pumps, and

59. Sewers being dug in Market Street in 1932, in preparation for the long-awaited mains water and sewage system opened in 1933.

for its sewage disposal on the regular visits of the night-soil collector. A report to the Parish Council in 1918 referred to *'the conditions prevailing in Wymondham at the present time are very bad (particularly with regard to water supply and sewerage), and a building scheme, however satisfactory with regard to the*

138

provision of decent houses, will be of little value unless a proper system is adopted'. A survey in 1919 revealed 130 houses as unsatisfactory and identified 20 for closure. It also said that *'scavenging* (e.g. night soil collection) *was little short of a scandal'*. In 1927 the Ministry of Health described the water supplies as most unsatisfactory and the Rural District Council gave the Parish Council permission to spend fifteen guineas on a preliminary report on water supply and sewerage.

Mains water and sewerage were eventually provided by the Forehoe Rural District Council in 1933, with the waterworks at High Oak, Wicklewood and the sewage works off Chapel Lane.

The first council houses were built by the RDC at Silfield Crescent in 1919, followed by Browick Road and Vimy Ridge, and, in the 1930s, by estates at Northfield, Silfield and Preston Avenue. Private house building was mainly in the form of sporadic development along the roads out of the town, particularly the Norwich Road, where houses were built on the north side in a scattered ribbon from Seymour House to the development at Norwich Common.

The state of the roads is indicated by the fact that in 1924 there was a deputation from the Parish Council to the County Council, eventually successful, to get the main London road through the town treated with tarmac granite and tarmac slag. The county council rejected an appeal for a speed limit, so the Parish Council asked the police *'to exercise strict supervision over the speed of motorists through the town'.*

The Wymondham Urban District Council was created in April, 1935 and took over the responsibilities of the former Forehoe RDC and the Parish Council, which was abolished. The first chairman was Edwin Gooch and the town clerk appointed was Lionel Standley, who was in the post for 39 years until the UDC was abolished in 1974. The UDC became responsible for the new water supply and sewerage systems and, as housing authority, took over nearly 200 council houses. It continued the council-house building programme and by 1938 had a total of 244 houses. The UDC was also responsible for the fire brigade and, after considerable public debate, made what was at the time a significant investment in a new Dennis fire engine to replace the old Victorian manual, horse-drawn – later lorry-drawn – pumps. One of the other new initiatives of the council was the construction of new toilets on the Market Place which, although largely underground, were a substantial intrusion into the open space.

In 1931 the population was 5,017.

60. The Market Cross in the 1920s.

Employment and Industry

Agriculture was still an important industry in the parish but throughout the inter-war years was in economic depression with unemployment and low wages. In 1923 there was a strike of agricultural workers over reductions in wages and increases in working hours. The strike lasted for four weeks and there was a mass meeting at Kimberley, where the strikers were supported by the Earl of Kimberley and addressed by George Edwards and Edwin Gooch. Wages were restored to wartime levels (a basic wage of 25 shillings) with no increase in hours. Despite undertakings of no victimisation, some workers did lose their jobs. The National Union of Agricultural Workers grew in numbers and influence. In 1925 there was a demonstration in Wymondham organised by the Union and the Labour Party where *'several thousand agricultural workers'* protested about the numbers of men out of work and the amount of land out of cultivation. Edwin Gooch, who became prominent in town affairs in the County Council and in Parliament, became its President in 1928. The General Strike of 1926 had its local impact, particularly affecting the railway services when most of the staff at the station joined the strike. Various schemes were suggested for providing work for the unemployed and in 1934 work started on creating a recreation ground on the former gravel pits in Browick Road. Progress was slow and not completed before the outbreak of war in 1939.

The brush factories were the major employers in the town. The Briton Brush Company was formed in 1920, taking over from S. D. Page and Sons and expanding in Factory Lane. There was a major fire in 1924, but the firm recovered, closed its factory in London in 1933 and concentrated all its manufacturing in Wymondham. It employed 400–500 workers, although its fortunes fluctuated with the economic recession in the 1930s and imports of cheap brushes from overseas. The company set up an engineering department with 30–40 engineers designing and making the specialist machinery for the factory. The Co-operative Society factory started in the Poynt Sawmills on Melton Road in 1922, making brushes for the Co-op. and employing over 200 workers. Smaller wood manufacturing concerns were Sam Kidman's factory in Vimy Ridge, Henry King's furniture factory at Browick Road and William Carter's brush factory in the former 'Dove' public house in Town Green. The Semmence family moved its coach-making business to Norwich Road before replacing it with a motor garage and a coach hire company.

In about 1914 the railway station had a considerable workforce: a station master, two foremen, six porters, four shunters, five signalmen, a pump operator, about ten goods and booking office clerks, level crossing staff, at least one engine driver and a firemen. In addition there were staff at the refreshment room and the W. H. Smith's bookstall.

In 1922 there were 12 trains daily to Norwich. The journey took 20 minutes on average, with some trains stopping at Hethersett and most at Trowse. There were 10 trains to London via Ely, which took about 3½ hours, and 6 trains to London via Forncett, which took between 3 and 4 hours. In addition there were 8 trains to Dereham, with through trains to Fakenham and Wells.

There was a considerable amount of goods and livestock traffic at the station, which had its own cattle pens. The brush factory of S. D. Page & Sons (later the Briton Brush Company) had its own siding from about 1916. In 1912 a siding was installed to serve the premises that later became Ayton Asphalt, and in 1920 this was extended to serve the adjoining King's Furniture Works. These sidings closed in the late 1960s.

Other important employers were the two laundries, which served a wide area around the town (including Norwich) and together employed over 150 workers. The Wymondham Laundry in Norwich Road started in 1912 and expanded substantially in the 1930s, while the Friarscroft Laundry started in the old weaving factory in Friarscroft Lane and moved to Melton Road in 1935. Corston's mineral water factory in Browick Road continued in production throughout the period, making up to 12,000 bottles of ginger beer and mineral waters per year and distributing them over half the country. The gravel industry, principally Ayton's, was thriving in the 1920s but declined seriously in the 1930s due to the national economic depression, despite the introduction of asphalt production in 1932. The cancellation of the national road programme caused serious financial problems for the company.

Schools

A major development was the opening of the new senior school on Norwich Road in 1938, built on a site which had been given to the town by C. R. Ayton as a sports field. (The proceeds were eventually put to the development of the recreation ground in Browick Road). The school at Norwich Common, which had only a small number of pupils, closed in 1935.

Social Life

The Town Hall ran at a loss from 1916 and eventually in 1920 was let out as a cinema. It still struggled to be viable and in 1923 the operator was granted a concession on his rent due to poor trade. Proprietors came and went. Then, in 1935, when an offer to purchase by Mr Spalding was agreed but later withdrawn, the company went into liquidation.

In addition to the cinema at the Town Hall, the Regal Cinema opened in Friarscroft Lane in 1937 and became very popular, with full houses every week and excited audiences at the Saturday morning children's shows. The covered swimming pool established in the old brewery in Brewery Lane in 1931 was one of only two in the county.

Up to the outbreak of war travelling fun fairs were held annually on the Fairland.

The Second World War

Before the outbreak of war the Urban District Council had prepared, under national guidance and instruction, for the possibility of hostilities. Thus in 1938 it set up an Air-Raid Precautions committee which was the focus for co-ordinating the ARP, Home Guard, Fire Service, First Aid organisations and nursing services. It was responsible for administering the reception and care of evacuees. Work started on public air-raid shelters in 1938 and by 1940 eleven were located at Priory Gardens, Damgate Street, Station Road, the Fairland, King's Head Meadow, the Windmill, Norwich Road, Folly Road and Cock Street. Shelters were built inside Browick School. In January 1939 there were 60 air-raid wardens and in the spring preparations were begun to receive evacuees. On 4th September, the day after war was declared, over 900 evacuees arrived in the town from Gravesend, after travelling by boat to Great Yarmouth. Many returned home in the period of the 'phoney war', but, after the blitz began on London, there was another influx and by September 1941 there were, officially, 965 in the town area. More evacuees came into the town in 1944–45 when V1 and V2 raids affected London and the Home Counties, even though several V2 rockets landed in Norfolk.

At the outbreak of war, the Territorial Army was mobilised and men, and later women, were called up for military or other service. They served in all the forces and many theatres of war, but particular groups of local men went to France with the British Expeditionary Force in 1939 (and left in the evacuation of Dunkirk). Others were in the reinforcements sent to Singapore in 1942 and taken prisoner by the Japanese.

The Local Defence Volunteers, later the Home Guard, were set up, with Wymondham as the headquarters for the 9th Battalion, Royal Norfolk Regiment, with a local company under the command of Major Phillip Fryer. A searchlight battery was stationed at Cavick. In 1941 the Council's 'Invasion Committee' gave advice to the public on action to be taken in the event of an invasion. In September 1942 it carried out a major exercise simulating an invasion by German forces involving service and other organisations

There were several air raids in the district in the first two years of the war, which caused relatively minor damage to a number of properties. In July 1942 there was a raid on the town when 200 incendiary bombs were recorded principally in the Fairland Street – Queen Street area, when the Baptist chapel was damaged. The town's fire brigade and other services were heavily involved in the fire-fighting and rescue operations in the Norwich blitz of 1942, when many people moved out

People of Wymondham !

WE are in the FOURTH Year of War.

A Wicked and Ruthless Enemy seeks to Destroy this Country.

The Peoples of the Occupied Countries— People like You, who lived in Towns like Yours—are Paying a Terrible Price because they were UNPREPARED FOR INVASION.

ANTI-INVASION Measures are intended to Protect the People.

BUT EVERYONE Must Know what to do if INVASION Comes.

It will be TOO LATE to Learn once the Enemy has Landed.

Those who could have Instructed you will be otherwise employed.

IT IS YOUR DUTY to Learn all you can about Anti-Invasion Measures NOW !

On September 20th

An INVASION EXERCISE

will be held in Wymondham.

This will be a rehearsal of what to do if the enemy lands.

Everyone MUST CO-OPERATE to the best of their ability so that the exercise will be a success.

We hope you will CO-OPERATE CHEER-FULLY.

GEO. R. REEVE, MODEL PRESS, WYMONDHAM, NORFOLK.

61. Preparing for the worst: a leaflet issued to the people of Wymondham in September 1942.

of the city to be housed in Wymondham and other places.

In 1942 the airfields at Hethel and Deopham (as elsewhere in the county) were under construction and in June 1943 Hethel was taken over by the 389th Bomb Group of the USAAF, flying B24 Liberators. Deopham was taken over by the 452nd Bomb Group early in 1944, flying B 17 Flying Fortresses. Large numbers of planes circling and assembling for the daylight raids on Germany became familiar sights in the skies over the town, with the planes returning later in the day, sometimes as squadrons and sometimes only in ones and twos.

The airfields attracted more enemy air activity and there were a number of attacks aimed at the airfields and returning aircraft.

A military hospital was set up, mainly in Nissen huts, at the former golf course at Morley in 1943. Casualties from the USAAF stations in East Anglia were treated there and in May 1944 the number of beds was expanded from 854 to 1,252 in anticipation of the invasion of Europe. After D-Day trainloads of wounded servicemen were received at Wymondham station and taken to Morley in convoys of ambulances. The hospital treated over 2,000 patients in 1944 and over 1,000 in1945. Rapid, post-operative, recovery techniques were pioneered.

From 1942 American servicemen became a very familiar part of the scene and the community. They are remembered particularly for the parties given for the schoolchildren and, especially by the girls, for the dances held on and off the bases. The Town Hall, which had been seriously damaged by fire in 1942, became the Anglo-American Club for Servicemen. The construction of the airfields made new demands for gravel from the town's pits.

After 1945

The Development of the Town

The second half of the twentieth century, from the end of the Second World War, saw the town's area expand and its population double, although the process was not a steady progression. For nearly twenty years after 1945, the town changed relatively slowly. The service establishments closed down and the US Air Force personnel had all gone by July 1945, although the sites were not sold off until the1950s. With the housing shortage in the late 1940s buildings on the airfields were occupied by 'squatters' for several years. The Morley hospital closed and its buildings were used until 1950 as an emergency teacher-training college. It was then acquired by the County Council to become its first boarding school.

In 1951 Wymondham's resident population was 5,665 (virtually the same as 100 years before) and by 1961 had reached 5,904.

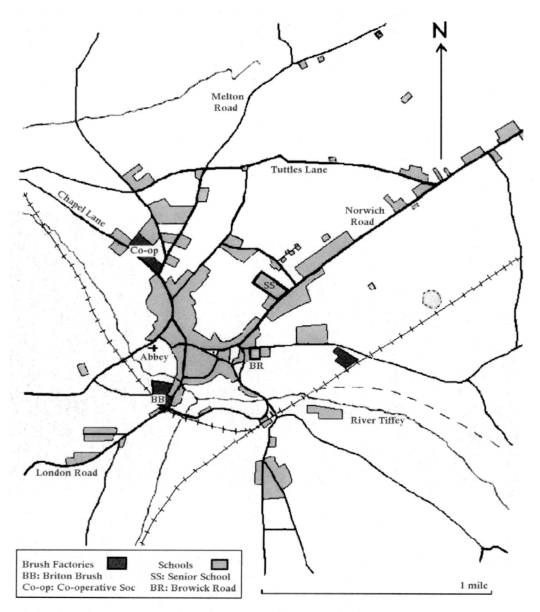

62. Map of the town of Wymondham in 1945.

The main concerns of the UDC as a housing authority were to maintain a house-building programme in response to the chronic post-war housing shortage and to exercise the new town-planning controls under powers delegated by the County Council. New building was concentrated mainly in the council housing estates. The inter-war estates were added to at Northfield, Silfield (including the prefabricated houses on Park Lane) and Preston Avenue, as, later, were the bungalow developments at Stanley Court and Ogden Close off Back Lane. Private housing was limited to infilling individual plots on Norwich Road and other roads north of the town centre. The first stage of a by-pass for the A11, from Bait Hill to the Fairland, was opened in 1958, relieving Damgate Street, Market Street and Bridewell Street of the trunk road traffic.

The recreation ground in Browick Road was brought into use. The Roman Catholic Church, built in Norwich Road, was dedicated as a national memorial to the Far East Prisoners of War. A major loss was the smock mill at Northfield which was destroyed by fire in 1950. It had been a feature of the landscape for nearly 100 years, retaining its sails although the machinery was motor powered.

63. A traffic jam in Damgate which remained part of the A11 trunk road until 1958.

The whole tempo of development changed in the mid-1960s, stimulated by the removal of the Lotus factory from Hertfordshire to the disused Hethel airfield in 1966. This created a demand for new housing from Lotus employees moving into the area. At the same time there was an upsurge in house building in the county. This was related to the growth in the economy and particularly to the expansion of Norwich, with Wymondham becoming more popular for commuters who worked in Norwich. While there was no formal plan to cater for this development, the Urban District Council, who exercised effective planning control at the time, resolved that new development should be contained within the area south of Tuttles Lane between the Norwich Road (then the A11) and Chapel Lane. In the 1960s the average number of new houses being built in the town was 115 per year

147

(compared with 60 per year in the previous ten years), the great majority built between the A11 and Chapel Lane. Within this development area the Robert Kett Middle School and Ashleigh First School were opened in 1968 and the High School (previously the Secondary Modern) expanded south of Folly Road. The population rose to 8,513 in 1971 and 9,759 in 1981.

Competition from buses and private cars saw a decline in the number of rail passengers from the 1930s and, therefore, in the 1950s and 1960s there were whole-scale closures in the Norfolk railway network. The line to Forncett closed in 1940 to passenger traffic and in 1951 to goods traffic. The line from Dereham to Wells closed in 1964, the line from Wymondham to Dereham in 1969 to passenger traffic and in 1989 to goods traffic. Wymondham station ceased to be staffed in the 1960s. The station buildings became neglected until taken over by David Turner in about 1990 and converted into the 'Brief Encounter' refreshment room and a piano showroom.

The second stage of the 'inner' by-pass, from the Fairland to Norwich Road, was built in 1968. The Central Hall, mainly financed by local subscriptions, was built and opened in 1965. A new police station was built by the Fairland in 1963 and a new fire station on the London Road in 1967. The old fire station became the entrance to a car park with the old upper storey retained on the Market Street frontage.

In 1962–63 there were proposals for the redevelopment of the south side of Market Street, involving two Georgian town houses, one associated with Cann's brewery (and then the Men's Club) and the adjoining timber-framed buildings, and the King's Head inn, which closed in 1962. The old properties were in a poor state of repair and, although listed and despite opposition, the UDC agreed to their demolition and redevelopment. New shops were built on Market Street, but the King's Head, acquired by Woolworth's, was only half demolished when the rebuilding was deferred. The site remained derelict until 1981, when the new store was completed.

Employment and Industry

Lotus, famous and successful with its Formula One racing cars, produced sports cars from 1966, including the 'Elan' in the 1970s and the 'Excel' and 'Esprit' in the 1980s. There were two divisions, one producing cars and the other providing an engineering consultancy which developed a world-wide reputation. After the death of its founder, Colin Chapman, the company was acquired by General Motors in 1976 and the 30,000th road car was built in 1984. The company experienced difficulties in the early 1990s and was bought by Bugatti in 1993, and then, in 1996, by the Malaysian company, Proton.

64. The historic King's Head inn shortly before demolition in the early 1960s.

New industrial estates were developed off Station Road, Silfield Road and Norwich Road. These were occupied mainly by a wide range of 'service' industries, but also by more specialised industries such as Vishay-Mann (making precision resistors), the Anglian Boiler centre, Pruce Newman (making all types of pipework) and Barley Chalu (aluminium coatings). Other significant employers were Barkers and Lee Smith (feedstuffs), Concrete Sections, Mann Components and Ayton Asphalt.

While the town and its economy were growing, the 1960s and 1970s saw the decline and eventual end of the brushmaking industry in the town. In the early post war years the brush firms were thriving and the Briton Brush Company exported worldwide, with agencies in over 30 countries. At one time the company accounted for 25% of the total export of brushes from the United Kingdom. The company was taken over by the Polycell Company of the Reed Group in 1967, and in 1973 the manufacture of paint brushes was moved to the Attleborough factory. The sawmills closed in 1976 and the factory was taken over by 'Windmill Brushes' but finally closed in 1985. The Co-op factory also declined and closed in 1987, when there were only 36 workers left. Both sites were redeveloped for housing.

65. Above the Georgian town houses.

Below the shops which replaced them.

Earlier, in the 1960s, the two laundries, which had been important employers before and just after the war, also closed. Corston's mineral water factory in Browick Road followed in 1977. In 1970 the Wymondham Laundry site in Norwich Road became the first large supermarket, originally 'Pricerite', in the county. It subsequently moved to the site near Tuttles Lane and is now the Waitrose store.

The Town Plans and Development

In 1971 the first plan for the development of the town was adopted by the UDC and the County Council. This defined the limits of development and included allocations for residential and industrial developments, and for the schools and open spaces. One of the issues, which recurred later, was the question of development west of Chapel Lane. Then, and later, the planning authorities refused proposals for building on the side of the Tiffey valley to preserve the open valley landscape and the long view to the Abbey.

In 1974 the South Norfolk District Council was created, taking over most of the responsibilities of the UDC and becoming the local planning authority. The Town Council became, for local government purposes, primarily a representative and consultative body with limited executive responsibilities. In 1979–80 the County Structure Plan identified Wymondham as an area for development associated with the growth of Norwich and, after local consultations, the new District Council produced a revision of the Local Plan for the town. This showed the main area for new housing, employment and open space development at Hart's Farm, south of the then A11. Although the Plan was adopted in 1988, there was a downturn in the national and local economies and development at Hart's Farm did not start until 1999. From that date housing development progressed steadily and by 2004 the residential development was substantially complete. In 2002 the County Police Headquarters were opened on the Gateway 11 Business Park and the recreation area at Kett's Field was brought into use. Further industrial and commercial development took place off Station Road and Silfield Road.

In 1994 the proposals for the outer A11 by-pass met strong opposition from environmental groups because of its impact on the countryside and particular concern at the effect on the Lizard, the only remaining common. The line was revised to skirt the Lizard and, with measures to protect the colony of great-crested newts, the road was completed in 1996. Archaeological investigations on the line of the road revealed an Iron Age complex at Silfield.

The Mid-Norfolk Railway Preservation Trust was established with a view to reopening the branch line between Wymondham and Dereham. The line was purchased in 1998 and passenger services have been run since 1999 by volunteers from a new halt close to the Abbey.

The Town Centre

The old streets of the town centre were designated a 'Conservation Area' in 1971 and the protection of the historic character of the town has been a major element of planning policy ever since. The District Council and other government agencies have contributed substantial sums in grant aid for the repair and restoration of many of the old buildings. However, in 1977 there was a public enquiry into proposals to demolish Rattle Row off Pople Street, a row of former weavers cottages built in the early nineteenth century, and permission was given for their demolition. They were replaced by bungalows for the elderly. The old weaving factory between Damgate and Chandlers Hill was demolished in 1973. The more enlightened and sympathetic approach to new development in the old town was demonstrated by the creation of the small shopping precinct at Wharton's Court (the former butcher's premises) and the housing development at Chandler's Hill. In the early 1990s there was much discussion over alternative schemes for reducing traffic through the town centre and giving greater priority for pedestrians, particularly in Market Street and on the Market Place, where the old underground toilets had been demolished in the 1970s.. Eventually the scheme of roadworks, traffic calming and control measures in Market Street, Bridewell Street, Damgate Street and Middleton Street, was put into effect from 1995. The character of shopping in the centre changed, as it did in many similar towns, with a reduction in the number of the independent food retailers, such as the butchers, bakers and grocers, and the introduction of non-retailing 'service' businesses, charity shops and catering establishments. Further links with the past were lost as the decline in the number of public houses continued (and one unfortunate change of name for one of the most historic) only partly offset by the increase in the number of restaurants and tea shops. The stall market on the Market Place revived in the 1980s but the dead stock market, which had moved to Station Road, finally closed.

A comprehensive project for the repair and restoration of the Market Cross was undertaken in 1988–89, which caused much concern when the exposed timbers were lime-washed in the traditional, but less fashionable, way.

Recreation and Health

One major project came to fruition in 1995–96. After many years of campaigning and fund raising, particularly by SWYM, a dynamic local committee formed by Denise Muir, the swimming pool, sports hall and fitness centre was opened near the High School in Norwich Road. This was a joint project of the District, County and Town Councils. SWYM revived an annual summer carnival in 1986, which continued under the Wymondham Lions for many years and is now a Fun Day.

In 1982 the local doctors' practice moved from Market Street to a new Health Centre on the former Saleground in Bridewell Street which has since become a centre for community health services, while the doctors' practice has moved to new premises at Postmill Close. There is a second doctors' surgery in Melton Road which is also seeking new premises.

Another landmark building was lost when the Women's Institute Hall on Norwich Road was demolished in 1965. While of little architectural merit, for 50 years it had played an important part in the cultural life of the town. However, one that has had a remarkable renaissance is the old railway station, taken over by David Turner for his piano business and part converted as 'The Brief Encounter Refreshment Room'. The station has become increasingly well used, particularly by commuters to Norwich and Cambridge. Although the Regal Cinema finally closed and became the Ex-Servicemen's Club, occasional films are shown by a voluntary group, 'The Regal Experience'.

The Bridewell ceased to be a police station in 1963 and its use as the Magistrates' Court finished in 1991. In 1994, after several years' fund-raising, the Wymondham Heritage Museum was established at the rear of the Council offices. After the Bridewell had been purchased by the Bridewell Preservation Trust in 1994, the Wymondham Heritage Museum was opened there in 1996. The Bridewell premises also provide accommodation for the Citizens' Advice Bureau, the Red Cross and community housing.

In the late 1990s and into the twenty-first century, the Town Council undertook several initiatives relating to the provision of outdoor recreation facilities. A new recreational area of 27 acres at Kett's Park (on Hart's Farm) was created for sports, with a woodland and picnic area, and a community centre. A riverside walk was opened from Damgate to Cavick and extended to Chapel Bridge. Footpaths and a nature reserve were created at Toll's Meadow, while a circular walk was opened at the Lizard.

The population of the district recorded in the 1991 census was 10,716 and in 2001 12,539.

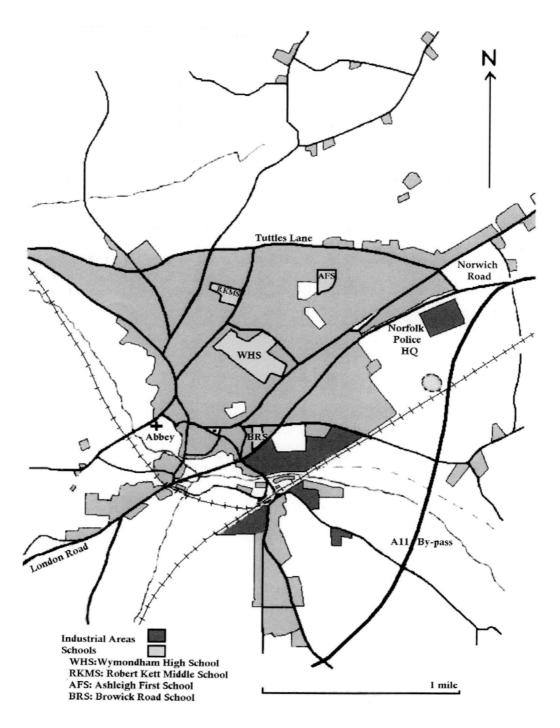

66. Wymondham: the town in 2000.

CHAPTER NINE

Postscript

The future

The new century has seen much discussion about more housing development in Wymondham. At the time of writing this is still in the pipeline. In the next hundred years the town may well have become much larger, as a satellite of Norwich, with only the historic town centre still recognizable. It will be interesting to see what happens.

There will undoubtedly be continuing pressures for new development and change, and Wymondham is likely to continue to be identified as a key location for development in the county. There is much more awareness and concern for the special character of the surrounding countryside than there was in the 1960s, but there will always be a need for those concerned to be vigilant and ready to respond to proposals which would damage that heritage.

Bibliography

General

F. Blomefield, *An Essay on the Topographical History of Norfolk* (1806)

The Reverend S. Martin Jones, *Wymondham and its Abbey* (1953)

J. E. G. Mosby & P. E. Agar, *Wymondham Old and New* (G. Reeve, 1949)

T. Ashwin & A. Davison, eds, *An Historical Atlas of Norfolk* (Phillimore, 2005)

Early Wymondham

Historical Environment Record (HER), Norfolk Museums Service

R. Bond, K. Penn & A. Rogerson: *The North Folk; Angles, Saxons and Danes* (Poppyland Publishing, 1990)

B. Robinson & T. Gregory, *Celtic Fire and Roman Rule* (Poppyland Publishing, 2003)

T. Williamson, *The Origins of Norfolk* (Manchester University Press, 1994)

Middle Ages

P. Brown, ed., *Domesday Book Norfolk*, 2 vols.(Phillimore, 1984)

B. Cornford, ed., *Studies towards a history of the Rising of 1381 in Norfolk* (1984)

D. C. Douglas, *William the Conqueror: The Norman Impact Upon England* (University of California Press)

W. Dugdale, *Monasticon Anglicanum*, iii, 330–1

L. Munby, 'How much is that worth?' (*British Association. for Local History*, 1996)

P. Maddern. *Imagining the Unchanging Land: East Anglians represent their Landscape, 1350–1500* in *Medieval East Anglia* edited by Christopher Harper-Bill 2005.

S. Schama, *A History of Britain* (2000)

J. Warrington, ed., *The Paston Letters* (1924)

K. Workman, 'Estate Administration in fifteenth-century Norfolk, based on the records of Grishaugh Manor, Wymondham' (University of East Anglia dissertation, 1995)

Website: Markets and fairs (www.history.ac.uk)

Sixteenth and Seventeenth Centuries

Norfolk Record Office: The Wymondham Town Book vols. 1, 2 & 3: MC2379, 965X2; ACC 2002/156; ACC 1997/240, (Transcripts in Wymondham Town

Archive). Drawings from Thomas Martin's notebook, Rye MS 17, Vol. IV, 1722.

C. Barringer, S. Spicer, eds, *Wymondham in the Seventeenth Century* (WEA, 1993)

E. Duffy, *The Stripping of the Altars* (London, 1992)

B. Garrard, *Wymondham Parish Gilds in the early Sixteenth century* (Reeves, 2003)

A. D. Hoare, *An Unlikely Rebel: Robert Kett and the Norfolk Rising 1549* (G. Reeves, 1999)

I. Roots, *The Great Rebellion 1642–1660* (London, 1966)

L. F. Salzman, *Building in England down to 1540* (Oxford, 1952)

A. H. Smith, *County and Court: Government and Politics in Norfolk 1558–1603* (OUP, 1974)

J. R. Tanner, *Tudor Constitutional Documents A.D. 1485–1603* (CUP, 1951)

W. E. Tate, *The Parish Chest* (Cambridge, 1983)

J. H. Wilson, ed., *Wymondham Inventories 1590–1641* (UEA, 1983)

Emigration

C. Barringer & S. Spicer, *Wymondham in the Seventeenth Century*

Registers of Passengers from Great Yarmouth to Holland and New England 1637–1639 (Norfolk Record Society, 1954)

J. Pound, *Tudor and Stuart Norwich* (Phillimore, 1988)

A. Taylor, *American Colonies – The Settlement of North America to 1800* (The Penguin History of the United States, Penguin, 2002)

Nonconformity

J. Ede & N. Virgoe, eds, *Religious Worship in Norfolk: the 1851 Census of Accommodation and Attendance at Worship* (Norfolk Record Society 1998)

J. Browne, *History of Congregationalism in Norfolk and Suffolk* (1877)

M. Scarborough, *Fairland United Reform Church 1652–2002, 350th Anniversary* (2002)

S. Weber Soros & C. Arbuthnott, *Thomas Jeckyll, Architect & Designer 1827–1881* (Bard Graduate Center, Yale, 2003)

The Eighteenth Century

John Barney: *The Defence of Norfolk 1793–1815* (Mintaka Books 2000)

J. Beresford (ed): *James Woodforde: The Diary of a Country Parson 1758–1802* (Canterbury Press 1996)

Anne Digby: *Pauper Palaces* (Routledge & Kegan Paul Ltd 1978)

Brian Fagan: *The Little Ice Age* (Basic Books, 2002)

W. Faden, pub., *A Topographical Map of the County of Norfolk* (1797; Lark's Press edition, 1989)

J. Gardiner,: *Urban Wymondham in the 1780s* (privately published, 1997)

N. Jenson: *Wymondham Bridewell: The Hidden Past* (Wymondham Heritage Society, 1997)

F. Meeres: *A History of Norwich* (Phillimore, 1998)

S. Wade-Martins & T. Williamson, eds, *The Farming Journal of Randall Burroughes 1794–1799* (Norfolk Record Society, 1995)

N. H. Williams, *The Oldest Law Firm in Norfolk* (Reeves, 1993)

B. Wilson, *The Contribution to Wymondham Abbey by the Reverend William Papillon* (Wymondham Abbey 2005)

Wymondham Town Archive,Wymondham Town Lands Charity accounts (copies and some originals)

Nineteenth and Twentieth Centuries

R. Adderson & G. Kenworthy, *Ely to Norwich* (Middleton Press 2002)

Bradshaw's July 1922 Railway Guide (David & Charles, reprint, 1985)

D. I. Gordon, *A Regional History of the Railways of Great Britain: The Eastern Counties* (David & Charles, 1990)

A. D. Hoare, *The Wymondham Story* (Wymondham Heritage Society, 2004)

P. Yaxley, *Memories of Old Wymondham* (Nostalgia Publications, Dereham, 1985)
P. Yaxley, *Wymondham – A Century Remembered* (Nostalgia Publications 1999)
P. Yaxley, *Wymondham and Attleborough in Old Photographs*

Other sources:

Wymondham Parish Records, Minutes of the Wymondham Vestry

Minutes of the Parish and Urban District Councils

Local newspapers including the *Eastern Daily Press* and *Norfolk Chronicle*

Picture and other Credits

The editors would like to thank the following individuals and organisations for permission to reproduce illustrations:

John Ayton: 8, 11, 33, 39, 41, 43, 44, 48*, 54, 62*, 64, 65, 66*

Chris Barringer: 1,2

Chris Barringer and John Wilson: 15

Suffolk Record Office, Bury St Edmunds: 17

Diderot's Enclyclopedie 1751-1780: 30

Mary Garner: 29, 34

Anne Hoare: 5, 37

Norfolk Archaeology Vol IX, 1884: 3

Norfolk County Council Library and Information Service: frontispiece, 27, 32a

Norfolk Museums and Archaeology Service: 4

Norfolk Record Office: drawings by Thomas Martin 1722 (RYE MS 17): 7,26, 31

Pepy's Library, Magdalene College, Cambridge: 18

John Wilson: cover, 9, 14, 16, 19, 21, 23, 24, 25, 28, 32b, 36, 51, 56

Wymondham Parish Records: 6

Wymondham Town Archive: 10, 12, 13, 20, 22, 35, 38, 40, 42, 45, 46, 47, 49, 50, 52, 53, 55, 57, 58, 59, 60, 61, 63

Maps marked with * are based on Ordnance Survey maps. reproduced by permission of Ordnance Survey on behalf of HMSO.
© Crown Copyright
All rights reserved
Ordnance Survey Licence Number 100032458

The quotes from the Wymondham Town Book are published with permission of Norfolk Record Office.
Books [1584]-1621, 1663-1772 and 1627-1663
Ref: MC 2379/3, 956x2; ACC 1997/240 and 2002/156 respectively

The editors have endeavoured to trace all copyright owners and apologise to anyone they have failed to contact.

Index